An ISO 9000 Approach to Building Quality Software

Östen Oskarsson
Systemkonsult

and

Robert L. Glass
Computing Trends

For book and bookstore information

http://www.prenhall.com

Prentice Hall PTR
Upper Saddle River, New Jersey 07458

Library of Congress Cataloging-in-Publication Data
Oskarsson, Östen.
    An ISO 9000 approach to building quality software / by Östen Oskarssson
    and Robert L. Glass
        p. cm.
    Includes index.
    ISBN 0-13-228925-3
        1. Computer software--Quality Control 2. ISO 9000 Series Standard   I. Glass,
    Robert L., 1932- . II. Title.
QA76.76.Q3504   1996
005.1'068'5--dc20   95-32815
                                      CIP

Editorial/production supervision
    and interior design: *Joanne Anzalone*
Manufacturing manager: *Alexis Heydt*
Acquisitions editor: *Bernard Goodwin*
Editorial assistant: *Diane Spina*
Cover design: *Anthony Gemmellaro*
Cover Design Direction: *Jerry Votta*
Art Director: *Gail Cocker-Bogusz*

The publisher offers discounts on this book when ordered in bulk quantities.
For more information, contact:
        Corporate Sales Department
        PTR Prentice Hall
        1 Lake Street
        Upper Saddle River, NJ 07458

        Phone: 800-382-3419, Fax: 201-592-2249
        E-mail: dan_rush@prenhall.com

Printed in the United States of America
10 9 8 7 6 5 4 3 2 1

ISBN 0-13-228925-3

Prentice-Hall International (UK) Limited, *London*
Prentice-Hall of Australia Pty. Limited, *Sydney*
Prentice-Hall Canada Inc., *Toronto*
Prentice-Hall Hispanoamericana, S.A., *Mexico*
Prentice-Hall of India Private Limited, *New Delhi*
Prentice-Hall of Japan, Inc., *Tokyo*
Simon & Schuster Asia Pte. Ltd., *Singapore*
Editora Prentice-Hall do Brasil, Ltda., *Rio de Janeiro*

Dedicated to

all those who work toward
the eventual inseparability
of the words "software" and "quality"

and especially to our wives
Maggan and Iris

CONTENTS

PREFACE

(Östen Oskarsson)

For many years I have taken part in software development projects, some of which have been successful and some of which have failed to meet deadlines or functional requirements. I love ISO 9000. Let me tell you why.

In 1987, two major companies, one in Sweden and one in Norway, were jointly purchasing a complex communication system from a well-known European supplier. According to the agreement, the supplier was to deliver the first installation one year after contract. When about half that time had passed, the supplier announced a delay, indicating software problems. The supplier now estimated the development time to be twice what the contract said (i.e., two years). This was when I was employed as a consultant by the customers to help them find out what the actual situation was with the supplier. We visited the supplier's software development site, and spent one week interviewing managers and software engineers and reading documentation.

The conclusion was clear: The project was out of control, and the new two-year estimate was not reliable. I helped the customers put pressure on the supplier, giving a long list of what had to be done about the project. The story had a relatively happy ending. The supplier reorganized and restarted the project, and came up with a credible time plan which ended up with a total project time of three years, three times what was contracted. At the cost of tripling the software effort, the supplier was also able to meet the three-year deadline and deliver on time.

This was the first time I had really seen the software problems with the *customer's* eyes, and I realized that almost all the shortcomings I had noted had to do with *management*, not technology. After I had presented my description of the supplier's shortcomings at a meeting, one of the programmers took me aside and said, "I'm very happy that you said what you did. We programmers have argued with management about this for years, but now perhaps something will happen." I realized that the problems I had seen when working myself with software had also mainly been managerial.

This is why I love ISO 9000. Its basic requirement is simply that there be adequate management of whatever activities are involved in creating products: don't promise what you can't meet; properly plan and manage development projects; and so on. If the customers mentioned above had forced the supplier to fulfill ISO 9000, or if the supplier on his own accord had chosen to work to the standard, there may still have been problems with the project, and there may have been errors in the product, but there would have been nothing at all like the total collapse we saw.

ISO 9000 is not necessarily the best way to put quality requirements on a software developing organization, and it must be used with care and intelligence when applied to software. But what is important is that it carries a lot of weight. The standard is widely accepted and used in almost all branches of industry throughout Europe and in many other parts of the world. Thus, when a customer includes a requirement for ISO 9000 in a contract, the supplier is unlikely to question it. If he does not already comply with the standard, he will probably not argue against the requirement.

When Bob Glass proposed this book as a joint project, I immediately became interested. I saw an opportunity to expand on some of my favorite hobbyhorses and, at the same time, hopefully give useful advice to software managers seeking ways to improve the capabilities of their organizations. Of course, I had previous acquaintance with Bob's impressive production of books about computing catastrophes and other entertaining subjects, as well as his more serious approaches to software engineering. I had especially enjoyed his book *Building Quality Software*, which I think gives much of the practical advise so many software managers are seeking. What I especially like is that his book avoids all the current talk about a software crisis, instead taking the positive approach of pointing to ways to improve software engineering still further.

I hope that our book will help software engineers and managers to improve their performance. Ideally, my text should provide a general understanding of quality systems in general and ISO 9000 in particular. The reader should then go on to Bob's wide-ranging and sometimes provocative text where the different options and issues involved with the actual *development* of software are explored. I see myself as the down-to-earth advisor relying on practical experiencee, discussing management, control, and other dull subjects. Bob is the provocative and free-ranging researcher, sharing with you his deep insight into the fascinating area of *doing* software development.

I have included a number of personal experiences in my text to illustrate my points. Also, reading about other's problems and mistakes tends to be fun. Remember that we should learn from the mistakes of others; life is too short for us to make them all ourselves. I hope you enjoy reading this book.

Östen Oskarsson

Spring 1995

PREFACE

(Robert L. Glass)

I first became aware of ISO 9000 and its impact on software in an unfortunate way. I had been brought to Helsinki to give a seminar on software quality to a Finnish audience, and in an early interaction one of the attendees asked me about a "Quality System." My response was to ask the attendee the same question with a slightly different inflection; "What *is* a Quality System?"

It slowly emerged from the ensuing discussion that the audience had come to the seminar seeking advice on how to build a Quality System as required by ISO 9000, and (because I had not yet heard of ISO 9000) my presentation was of little help to them in that regard!

There wasn't much I could do to recover from that debacle at the seminar, but I made a point of trying to get smarter about ISO 9000 shortly after I returned home. With the help of some European colleagues, including Östen Oskarsson of Sweden, I began to gather the information—and the documentation—that I needed for my learning experience.

But there was still a problem. The more I read about ISO 9000, the less interested in it I became. My interest in software quality has always been from the technical point of view. I strongly believe that the task of building a quality software product belongs to technologists and only peripherally to managers and, in fact, that management's typical role of pressuring technologists to put quality into the product is really counterproductive. I agree with Tom DeMarco, who says that the competent software professional inherently wants to build a quality product, and management's appropriate role is to remove the barriers that prevent him or her from doing so.

Yet the quality viewpoint taken by ISO 9000 is solidly in the quality management camp rather than the quality technology camp. ISO 9000 contains a lot of "thou shalts" and little technical advice on how to accomplish what it requires. Furthermore, my view of what it contained, at that early stage in my ISO 9000 knowledge-gathering, was that its "thou shalts" were pretty superficial. They might (or might not) assist the software technologist in building a quality product, but they didn't get at the essence, the technology, of quality.

Time passed, and I resisted getting any further interested in ISO 9000. But as that time passed, my European colleagues got more and more involved in the application of ISO 9000 to software, and it soon became apparent that the standard was beginning to spread across the Atlantic as well. For example, in [Yourdon 1994] the author said things like "How does [a software company] inspire confidence when it makes such claims as ... 'we deliver high quality software'? ... By achieving level-5 SEI status, and by achieving ISO 9000 certification." Another writer worth reading, P. J. Plauger [Plauger 1995], said, "ISO 9000 as a selling point depends largely on your customers. Those who demand it will settle for no less..." As author of the book *Building Quality Software* (Prentice Hall, 1992) and a lecturer on the material it contained, I realized that I could ignore the standard no longer.

Meanwhile, Östen Oskarsson contacted me about some book projects—he had written a Swedish-language book on

small software projects, and was interested in the possibility of my helping translate it into American (!)—and we
renewed our discussion of ISO 9000. Östen was involved in
more and more ISO 9000 consulting work, and was becoming more and more convinced of its value. Since over the
years I have come to believe in Östen's beliefs—his Ph.D.
thesis was an impressive case study of an early industrial
object-oriented software project, for example (Sweden pioneered the application of OO approaches at the communication company Ericsson)—I was prepared to listen when
Östen discussed ISO 9000.

Following Östen's interest, I took another look at the
standard, discussed my reservations with him, and committed to working with him to write this book. We decided
on a division of labor that relied on Östen's expertise to
present and discuss the standard itself, and my background in the technology of software quality to bridge the
gaps between what the standard required and what building quality software (in my view, at least) is really all
about. And we made one other decision. This book, our
book, would be written as a companion to *Building Quality
Software* (*BQS*). That is, for the reader who already knew
what was in *BQS*, this new book could stand alone. But for
the reader who was still struggling with how to achieve
quality software, this book would present ISO-9000-
related information, but refer broadly to *BQS* for the
details and references necessary to translate ideas into
implementations. In other words, if the treatment of a
topic in this book is too terse, the reader is encouraged to
refer to the same topic in *BQS*, where the treatment would
be more complete.

In fact, that was the reason for the title of this book. *An
ISO 9000 Approach to Building Quality Software* has two
meanings: to provide guidance to those who want to build a
quality software product, of course, but also as a supplement
to *BQS* that makes it relevant to ISO 9000.

That was the platform upon which we began to erect the

structure of this book, and we have continued on that platform, largely unchanged. As I reread ISO 9000 in order to do
this book, however, I began to gain a new appreciation for
what it was really about. I believe there are three things
about the standard that one must understand in order to
appreciate it:

1. It is a tool for customers *buying* software more than for
   developers *building* it.

2. It is about what, not how. The standard requires that certain goals be achieved, but it says little about how to
   achieve them.

3. It is about things that are necessary, but by no means
   sufficient. The standard requires that a number of important goals be achieved, but the achievement of those
   goals does not ensure that a quality software product will
   result.

The first two points above, I believe, are ones with which
most ISO standards enthusiasts would agree. The third may
be more problematic. There is a clear implication throughout
the standard that following its dictates will ensure a quality
product.

There are two problems with ISO 9000 that account for
this difference of opinion, I believe:

1. The standard was defined by quality people. That is, the
   originators of the standard knew a lot about quality, but
   little about the discipline to which it is applied. This is
   particularly problematic with software, a discipline so
   unusual that its product has no weight, costs nothing to
   manufacture, is created by brainpower, and requires no
   raw materials to produce.

2. The standard was originated in the manufacturing
   world. In that world, "what" is more easily translated

into "how," and the gap between necessary and sufficient is (by contrast) relatively small. What is complicated about manufacturing disciplines is often the process of manufacturing itself. But in software, the complication lies in analysis and design, and manufacturing is trivial.

Thus, the fertile field that gave rise to ISO 9000 could not have been further from the needs of software. Even the attempts to make the standard relevant to software—ISO 9000-3 and some of the national approaches to interpreting the standard, such as England's TickIT—could not fill the gap between what and how, and between necessary and sufficient. This gap has been noted elsewhere; for example, in [Avison 1994].

It was the task of filling that gap that Östen and I set out to fulfill.

In the final analysis, here is what I believe Östen and I have accomplished in this book. Östen, knowledgeable in the what and why of the standard, has done an excellent job of sharing with the reader what the standard is, how it is to be applied, where it stands in the overall world of software quality approaches, and what has happened in specific applications of the standard. I personally find his "war stories," for example, a high point—and a major contribution—of this book.

What I hope I have accomplished, on the other hand, is a narrowing of the gaps between what and how, and necessary and sufficient. Given that I believe adherence to the standard does *not* necessarily guarantee a quality software product, I have tried to provide the insight needed to supplement the standard and improve its chances of accomplishing what its originators wanted it to achieve.

The resulting book may represent something of an odd couple: Östen describing ISO 9000 and its benefits, and me chiding the standard and trying to offer what it does not! I hope those differences do not significantly bother the reader, because I believe that the result is a blend that will make ISO 9000 truly useful, the standard that it was intended to be all along. It all reminds me of that wonderful little book *The Elements of Style* by Strunk and White, a classic in the field of English and writing. In that book, Strunk is the pedantic instructor, laying out terse stylistic rule after terse stylistic rule, and White is the master stylist, exhibiting what writing with style really means. The book moves schizophrenically from Strunk's part I to White's Part II. But the whole is a magnificent blend of what the reader needs to know to write with style.

It is presumptuous to even wish that this book could be for software quality what *The Elements of Style* is for writing. The classic contribution of Strunk and White is too massive to be belittled by weak analogy. But you understand what I am trying to say. Given that Östen and I bring very different things to the ISO 9000 table, I hope these things blend well in this book.

In the final analysis, you are the judge.

References

[Avison 1994] D. E. Avison, H. U. Shah, and D. N. Wilson "Software Quality Standards in Practice: The Limitations of Using ISO-9001 to Support Software Development," *Software Quality Journal,* 3, 105–111, 1994.

[Plauger 1995] P. J. Plauger, "Playing it Safer," *Embedded Computer Systems,* Jan. 1995.

[Yourdon 1994] Ed Yourdon, *Guerilla Programmer,* p. 3, Sept. 1994.

Robert L. Glass

Spring, 1995

ABOUT THE
AUTHORS

Östen Oskarsson is currently running his own one-man consultancy firm in Linköping, Sweden, specializing in quality assurance of software development and maintenance. Assignments include support to software suppliers regarding methods and management; support to the customer side of software acquisitions; and ISO 9001 certification of software organizations. Dr. Oskarsson has been working in the European software industry for 15 years, first employed at the communications system supplier Ericsson and the defense system group FFV, and later as a consultant. Beginning in 1987, he has conducted about 100 software quality audits of European organizations to ISO 9001 and other standards.

Östen Oskarsson received a Ph.D. in computer science from Linköping University in 1982, and he became a registered TickIT auditor in 1993. Dr. Oskarsson is the author of two Swedish books: *Software Quality Assurance* (with Christer v Schantz), Industriförlaget, 1990, and *Small-Scale Software Development*, Studentlitteratur, 1994.

Robert L. Glass is President of Computing Trends, publishers of *The Software Practitioner.* He has been active in the field of computing and software for over 40 years, largely in industry but also as an academic. In industry, he has managed projects, built and maintained software for most application domains, and engaged in research and development. In academe, he taught for five years in the software engineering graduate program at Seattle University, was a visiting professor for several summers at Linköping University in Sweden, and spent a year at the Software Engineering Institute at Carnegie-Mellon University.

He is the author of 19 books and 49 published papers on computing and software, editor of the *Journal of Systems and Software,* publisher and editor of *The Software Practitioner,* and was for 15 years a Lecturer for the Association for Computing Machinery. He received an honorary Ph.D. from Linköping University, Sweden, in 1995.

Regarding software quality, Glass has taught seminars on the subject in industry, taught a course on the subject at Seattle University, and written three previous books on the subject:

Building Quality Software, Prentice Hall, 1992

Measuring Software Design Quality, with David N. Card, Prentice Hall, 1990

Software Reliability Guidebook, Prentice Hall, 1979

ISO 9000 AND SOFTWARE

BACKGROUND ON ISO 9000

1.1 BUYING NUTS AND BOLTS

A friend of mine makes a living out of buying and selling nuts and bolts. He buys large quantities from suppliers in southeast Asia and then distributes them to his customers in Scandinavia. I was intrigued to learn that the difficult part was not the selling, that is, getting rid of the stuff at a profit; it is *buying* the nuts and bolts.

My friend would receive a few lorries loaded with bolts and nuts every now and then. If they were faulty in any way, he was in trouble. For example, the dimensions might be wrong, or the steel quality, or the threading. He would then be unable to deliver to his own customers, and thus—no profit (rather the opposite).

"But," I said, "surely you could claim damage from the suppliers." "Possibly," my friend answered, "but if I had lost my customers, that would not help very much. I cannot live on damage, I must do business."

So, the solution for my friend was to put additional requirements on his suppliers. He would specify dimensions, steel quality, threading, and so on in the contract. Further-

3

more, he would specify requirements on the internal workings of the supplier companies in order to ensure that what was delivered would be what his customers needed. He would impose requirements on a supplier's purchasing of material, manufacturing process, quality control, and checking procedures. If he were satisfied that the supplier would buy the right kind of raw material, use a reliable manufacturing process, and perform sufficient checks on the products, my friend would be able to sleep at nights while waiting for the delivery.

My friend states these "extra" requirements by requiring that the supplier fulfill the requirements in an ISO 9000 standard. ISO 9000 is a set of standards intended for just my friend's kind of needs. They specify requirements on the supplier's organization and procedures intended to give the customer confidence in the products to be delivered.

1.2 THE ISO 9000 FAMILY OF STANDARDS

The International Organization for Standardization (ISO) is a worldwide federation of national standards bodies such as the American National Standard Institute (ANSI). ISO prepares international standards, which are publicized after voting among ISO members.

ISO 9000 is a family of standards and guidelines. Figure 1.1 shows some ISO 9000 documents which may be of interest for us.

The document ISO 9000-1 is a general guideline which gives background information about the family of standards.

ISO 9001, ISO 9002, and ISO 9003 are the *standards* in the family, containing requirements on a supplier. ISO 9002 and ISO 9003 are subsets of ISO 9001. ISO 9002 is used for situations in which there is no design. ISO 9003 is used in situations in which there is neither design nor production

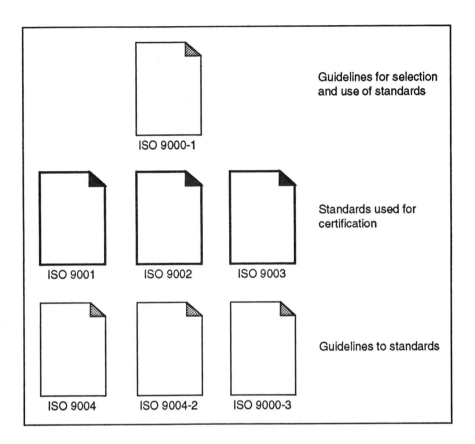

Figure 1-1

(e.g. retail). For software development, ISO 9001 is the standard to use.

ISO 9004 is a comprehensive guideline to the use of the ISO 9000 standards. ISO 9000-3 is a guideline on how to use ISO 9001 for software development. ISO 9004-2 is a guideline for the application of ISO 9001 to the supply of services. It may be of interest in the context of IT, since computer centers and other suppliers of data services can benefit from its advice.

In the United States, the ISO 9000 standards may be obtained from either the American Society for Quality Control (ASQC) or ANSI at these addresses:

American Society for Quality Control
P.O. Box 3006
Milwaukee, WI 53201-3006
Phone: 414-272-8575
Fax: 414-272-1734

American National Standards Institute
11 West 42nd Street
New York, NY 10036
Phone: 212-642-4900
Fax: 212-398-0023

1.3 ISO 9001

1.3.1 GENERAL

Since software production is mostly a question of design, ISO 9001 is the standard of interest for us. Its title is "Quality systems—Model for quality assurance in design, development, production, installation and servicing". Don't focus too much on the word "quality" in the title. ISO 9001 is about *management*. It contains requirements on how a company shall be managed on different levels and from different aspects. It most definitely does not include requirements on *products*.

Roughly, we might say that ISO 9001 puts only two basic requirements on a supplier:

1. All operations influencing quality shall be under control.

2. This control shall be visible.

Of course, the standard puts these requirements in much more detail and many more words, but these two requirements capture the essence of ISO 9001.

The second requirement is usually formulated as a

requirement that plans, procedures, organization, and so on be documented, and that important activities be recorded.

ISO 9001 expects fairly strict organization, where managers have the responsibility and authority to control the work of their subordinates. Self-organizing groups are difficult to fit into the requirements of ISO 9001.

ISO 9001 is written for the manufacturing industry. To apply the standard to software development requires a certain amount of interpretation.

The first version of ISO 9001 was published in 1987. Versions of ISO standards are defined by the year of publication, so that version was defined as ISO 9001:1987. In mid-1994, version 2 of the standard was published, not surprisingly called ISO 9001:1994, and this book is about that version. The differences between versions 1 and 2 are relatively minor. To a large extent, the new version makes explicit some things one had to deduce from the earlier version.

1.3.2 ISO 9001 AND DOCUMENTATION

ISO 9001 is very insistent about documentation. Procedures shall be documented, and records shall be prepared and kept for most of what goes on inside the company. This has caused many managers to fear the standard. They have nightmares about mountains of paper and a bureaucratic organization, where filling out forms takes more time and is more important than producing goods. They are right. Improper use of the standard can easily introduce unnecessary complexities, which can make a supplier inferior in comparison to the situation before ISO 9001. This danger is especially pronounced if the standard is enforced by bureaucratic personalities who mistake paper for results.

I frequently fight quality managers whose main argument is "We must do this because it says so in the standard." "But will it make you a better supplier?" I ask. "But it says so in the standard" is the irrelevant answer. The key question to ask in this situation is why a standard would enforce something that does not make you a better supplier. If this specific paperwork does not benefit you and does not benefit your customers, why would anyone in his or her right mind want it?

1.3.3 THE RISK FOR BUREAUCRACY

Please notice an important word in the title of ISO 9001: "Model." All of the requirements in the standard do not necessarily have to be taken literally. If, in your company, there is a simpler way to achieve the same thing as the ISO 9000 requirement intended, well, good for you!

Notice that often there are two ways to meet a requirement in ISO 9001:

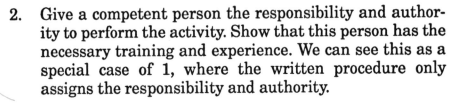

1. Issue a written procedure for the activity, and check that the procedure is followed.

2. Give a competent person the responsibility and authority to perform the activity. Show that this person has the necessary training and experience. We can see this as a special case of 1, where the written procedure only assigns the responsibility and authority.

I heard about an extreme case the other day. The owner of a small company manufacturing specialized ultra-high-precision custom instruments wanted to show that his company fulfilled ISO 9001. However, he refused to issue detailed procedures. He claimed that he only hired extremely well qualified staff, with solid education, long experience, and excellent references. "To throw detailed instructions at them would be insulting and counterproductive, and I will not do it," he was reported to say.

So he documented his method of controlling his company, describing what responsibility and authority he had given to his employees. He also documented his own means for knowing that excellent products were produced. He then brought in some third-party auditors to assess the company's compliance with ISO 9001. The assessors shook their heads at the sight of the slim documentation handed them as a definition of the "quality system" of the company. They then spent considerable time trying to find holes in the quality system. In the end, they had to give up. You see, the question they were asking themselves the whole time was, "Can we see that this activity is under control?" And then they found that there was brief but exact documentation of the control, and they could see in the workshops that the work was actually controlled and performed in this way.

Creating rules and formality in order to fulfill ISO 9001 is rather like balancing on an edge. On one side is the dangerous swamp "Bureaucracy," which can clog your activities forever, and on the other side is the slippery hillside "Happy-go-lucky", where you don't know what will happen.

Figure 1-2 is an attempt to illustrate this phenomenon. The Y axis represents quality and productivity. The X axis represents formality and paper work. Too little formality and

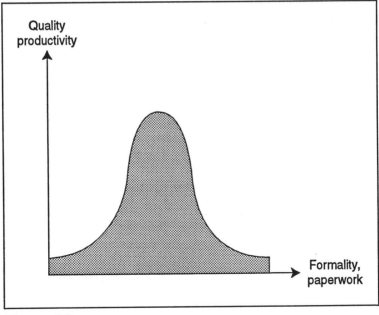

Figure 1-2

paperwork leads to low quality and productivity, since the developers make errors and repeat work done in other projects (e.g., on development methods). Too much of it also leads to low quality and productivity, since the most effort goes into following rules and doing paperwork. If a software development organization finds the *right* level of formality and paper work there is an optimum, which will give very high quality and productivity.

However, I sometimes see how organizations find themselves to the left in Figure 1-2. Management realizes that something has to be done about software development. Perhaps some people are available who have not done too well with software development, and management must find some other use for them. Chances are that management will give these people the task of defining procedures and standards for software development. Alternatively, an external consultant may be called in to do the job. In either case, after a while the organization will probably find itself in the right-hand side of Figure 1-2. Two or three thick binders with rules and standards have been produced, and management is trying to enforce them; and neither quality nor productivity have improved. Very soon, the developers stop trying to use the rules, and then the managers say: "Software developers are creative artists who can't be controlled. Let's leave them alone." And the software engineers say: "You can't have rules for software development; we must each, in each case, decide how to work."

1.3.4 QUALITY AUDITS AND OBJECTIVE EVIDENCE

Let us look into two closely linked concepts that are central to ISO 9001: *quality audits* and *objective evidence*.

"*Quality audit:* A systematic and independent examination to determine whether quality activities and related results comply with planned arrangements and whether these arrangements are implemented effectively and are suitable to achieve objectives." (ISO 8402-1986, "Quality—Vocabulary")

A quality audit of an organization is when somebody independent of the manager of that organization checks whether rules and procedures are followed, and whether the rules and procedures lead to the intended result. A first-party audit is when the audit is conducted by or on the behalf of company management. First-party audits cover the different parts of a company, but not the company as a whole (nobody inside the company would be independent enough). A second-party audit is when a customer conducts an audit of some part or all of a supplier's operation. Third-party audits are conducted by independent external auditors.

A central concept in auditing is "objective evidence." When a customer or a third-party auditor comes to a company to see whether it fulfills ISO 9001, they must be able to see what has been done prior to the visit. Therefore, if, for example, the supplier's procedures require that a review or check be performed, ISO 9001 requires documented evidence of the review or check. For example, I might ask a manager, "Has this inspection been done?" The answer is, "Oh yes!"

"How do you know?"

"Charlie in the workshop told me the other day that he had made that inspection."

I would not accept that answer; hearsay is not enough for ISO 9001. If, however, I were shown a document saying that Charlie did the inspection of item x according to procedure y and found z, signed Charlie and dated, I would believe it. That document would constitute objective evidence.

How do we know that Charlie did not fake it and sign the document, and what it says is not true? Of course, we can't know this with absolute certainty. However, in general, people are reluctant to put their signatures on something clearly a lie. Personally, I have not been able to find any cases where a person has signed a statement he or she knew to be false in many years of auditing experience.

1.3.5 THE CONCEPT OF THE QUALITY SYSTEM

ISO 9001 contains requirements on a supplier's *quality system*. According to ISO, a quality system comprises "the organizational structure, responsibilities, procedures, processes and resources for implementing quality management."

This is an important concept, and it is frequently misunderstood. When I come to audit a supplier, sometimes the quality manager gives me a binder and proudly states, "This is our quality system." Paper can only be part of a quality system; it also includes such things as people, equipment, competence, practices, and so on.

In a software development organization, the quality system may consist, for example, of:

- The quality policy
- The organization
- The staff
- The competence of the staff
- The quality manual
- Written procedures
- Checklists
- Records (e.g., minutes of meetings, test records)
- Common practices

1.3.6 TWENTY QUALITY ELEMENTS

The meat of ISO 9001 is placed in its Chapter 4, which is subdivided into 20 paragraphs:

4.1   Management responsibility

4.2   Quality system

4.3   Contract review

4.4 Design control

4.5 Document and data control

4.6 Purchasing

4.7 Control of customer-supplied product

4.8 Product identification and traceability

4.9 Process control

4.10 Inspection and testing

4.11 Control of inspection, measuring and test equipment

4.12 Inspection and test status

4.13 Control of nonconforming product

4.14 Corrective and preventive action

4.15 Handling, storage, packaging, preservation and delivery

4.16 Control of quality records

4.17 Internal quality audits

4.18 Training

4.19 Servicing

4.20 Statistical techniques

The subject of each paragraph is called a *quality element,* defined by the paragraph headline. These quality elements are household concepts in the world of quality assurance. In particular, quality auditors, who specialize in assessing conformance to ISO 9000 standards, will frequently refer to the quality elements when discussing conformance. Also, they tend to have a common understanding of what is needed in order to fulfill each quality element.

In Chapter 3 of this book, we will look into each quality element in turn.

1.4 CERTIFICATION TO ISO 9001

1.4.1 BACKGROUND

ISO 9001 is intended to be used in a contract between a customer and a supplier. However, a growing use of the standard is also for *certification*.

When customers started including ISO 9001 in contracts, they realized that they had to convince themselves that the supplier actually fulfilled the requirements of the standard. It was not enough just to include a reference to the standard in the contract; if the supplier failed to fulfill ISO 9001, you might be able to sue them for breaking the contract, but this would not give you your nuts and bolts or whatever you had contracted. So customers started to conduct *quality audits* on the supplier's premises, looking into the methods of management and also spot-checking ongoing activities and comparing them with the requirements of the standard. Quality audits were part of both the precontract assessment of suppliers and the continuing supervision of the selected supplier.

If a supplier has many customers, it would become costly and awkward to have all of them visiting the supplier for a few days each to convince themselves that the supplier is fulfilling the requirements of ISO 9001. Customers' audits would also occupy key staff, and thereby risk disrupting the actual performance of contracts.

Then someone had a bright idea: Why not have only one party investigate the supplier and issue a certificate, which the supplier would then use as a simple way to convince all customers that the standard is fulfilled? This would make ordinary quality audits by the customers unnecessary. Thus, the scheme of ISO 9000 certificates was born.

Today, a large number of European and other countries' industries can show certificates of their compliance with ISO 9000 standards. Customer audits have become rare, but there is still a need for them because:

- An ISO 9000 certificate is only a simple "yes" to the question of compliance. In order to compare different suppliers, the customers still have to look into it for themselves.

- Especially for new technical areas (e.g., software) judgments vary widely between certification bodies depending on the competence of the auditors and the choice of interpretation of the standard.

Still, there are cases now in Europe where you would not be welcome to tender a bid if your company were not certified to the appropriate ISO 9000 standard.

1.4.2 THIRD-PARTY CERTIFICATION

A number of companies specialize in certification of suppliers to ISO 9001 and other standards. This is called *third-party certification,* and the certifying company is a *certification body.* Such companies sell only one commodity, the service of assessing conformance to standards, combined with the issuing of certificates for those customers who actually fulfill the requirements of the applicable standard.

A third-party certification of a supplier to ISO 9001 might consist of the following steps:

1. The supplier invites bids from several certification bodies.

2. The supplier agrees on a contract with one certification body. The selection criteria are usually price, reputation, and competence in the supplier's business area.

3. The certification body makes a thorough study (audit) of the supplier's rules, practices, organization, documentation, and so on, and raises nonconformance notes on aspects which are not up to ISO 9001.

4. When the supplier has shown that the nonconformances

are corrected, the certification body issues a certificate saying that the supplier fulfills the requirements of ISO 9001.

5. Thereafter, the certification body will regularly (e.g., twice a year) make follow-up audits to check that the certificate is still valid.

6. The certificate expires after three years, when a new certificate must be issued. Under certain circumstances, the certification body is obliged to withdraw an existing certificate immediately, for example, if the supplier is using the certificate improperly in its marketing, implying that the *products* have been certified to ISO 9001.

1.4.3 WHO IS WATCHING THE WATCHERS?

Since the certification body is paid by the supplier to issue a certificate that is important for that supplier, isn't there a risk that the certification body will be too lenient because they want to keep the supplier as a customer? A less serious certification body might perhaps even specialize in selling budget-priced certificates.

Actually, the certification business seems to work fine in Europe. This is because the value of a certificate depends on how strongly the supplier's own customers value it. This, in turn, mainly depends on the reputation of the certification body. In this way, then, there is definite pressure on the certification bodies not to be lenient. It would be very unpleasant for a certification body if the supplier's customer phoned and said, "How could you certify that company? I contracted them because they were certified, but they bungled the contract and the product is useless!" If rumors of such occasions started to circulate, the certification body would find itself out of business.

Also, most certification bodies are *accredited* in the countries where they operate. National accreditation authorities establish the rules for each certification body, and in what business areas each may issue ISO 9000 certificates. The accreditation authorities monitor all accredited certification bodies continuously, for example, by observing their practices during actual certifications. The accreditation authority in the United States is the Registrar Accreditation Board (RAB). The RAB uses a terminology that differs somewhat from that of Europe. A certification body is a *registrar*, and certification is registration. In this book, we stick to the European terms *certification body* and *certification*, since those are well established in most of the world. Figure 1-3 summarizes the relation between accreditation and certification.

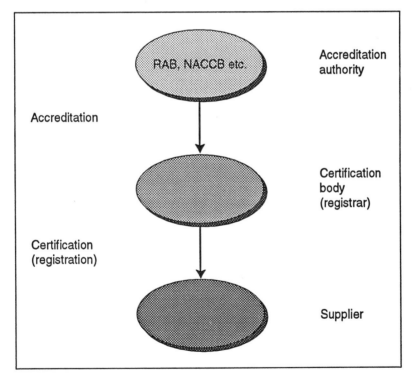

Figure 1-3

Certification bodies accredited in Europe work under ISO 10011, "Guidelines for auditing quality systems," "Part 1: Auditing" and "Part 2: Qualification criteria for quality system auditors"; and under EN45012, "General criteria for certification bodies operating a quality system." RAB uses other means to formulate requirements on certification bodies in the United States.

The Use of ISO 9001 with Software Development

2.1 Manufacturing Industry vs Software Industry

The ISO 9000 standard with which we are concerned is ISO 9001, since it applies to "quality assurance in design, development, production, installation and servicing." As mentioned above, this standard is written for the manufacturing industry, and this poses some problems when applying it to the development and maintenance of software.

In what way, then, is software different? Figure 2.1 illustrates manufacturing and software development from this perspective. The rectangles symbolize cost or effort.

If we first look at manufacturing, for example, kettles, we see that *design* is a relatively minor activity. Instead, the cost for each manufactured item is notable, so when a few items have been produced, *production* is by far the major part of the activity. Therefore, when we talk about quality or productivity problems and improvements in manufacturing, we tend to focus on production.

Software development, however, is nearly 100% *design*. Production means to copy executable code to diskettes, tapes, or ROMs, and is performed and checked automati-

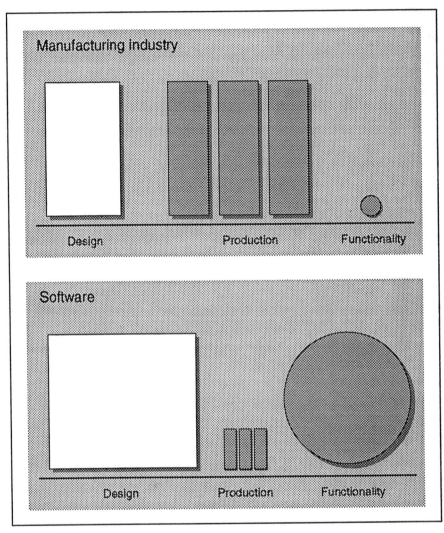

Figure 2-1

cally. So, when talking about quality and productivity, we focus on design.

Another difference is illustrated by the circles to the right of the figure. The functionality and complexity of software and complex electronics are many orders of magnitude greater than those of ordinary appliances. Actually, in my opinion, today's software products are the most complex items created by humanity, with the exception of our civilizations. Thus, the need for control is greater in software development than in the production of appliances; at the same time, that control is more difficult to define and apply.

ISO 9001 covers design, but it focuses on production. Even for a production expert, the text in the standard is brief and needs explanation. In order to apply it to software development, the standard must be interpreted and explained still further. Chapter 3 gives such interpretations and explanations.

2.2 ISO 9000-3

The need for a special interpretation of ISO 9001 for software was noted quite early, and in 1991 ISO published a guide for this purpose. The guide is numbered ISO 9000-3, and its title is "Quality management systems—Part 3—Guideline for the application of ISO 9001 to the development, supply and maintenance of software."

This document is a *guideline*, not a standard. It incorporates some parts of ISO 9001 verbatim, and in those parts the word "shall" is used. In the rest of the text, the word "should" is used.

Even though ISO 9000-3 is a guideline and uses "should," it has a special status. It is not just any guideline; it is ISO's own authorized guideline to the use of ISO 9001 with software. Thus, ISO 9000-3 is occasionally used as a requirement standard in the same manner as is ISO 9001. In those cases, "should" is taken to mean "shall."

ISO 9000-3 is only one of many possible interpretations of ISO 9001 for software. It is possible to fulfill ISO 9001 without fulfilling every "should" in ISO 9000-3. However, if there is a "should" in ISO 9000-3 that you do not fulfill, you should be prepared to explain to an auditor how you handle that issue, and why you still believe you fulfill ISO 9001.

ISO 9000-3 is not organized in quality elements; instead, the guideline is organized into three main groups. The first group contains general requirements on the company and its management. The second group contains requirements on projects and the maintenance phase. The third group contains requirements on "supporting activities," that is, activities independent of phases. The three groups are documented in Chapters 4, 5 and 6, respectively, of ISO 9000-3. The table of contents of these chapters is as follows:

4 QUALITY SYSTEM FRAMEWORK
    4.1   Management responsibility
    4.2   Quality system
    4.3   Internal quality system audits
    4.4   Corrective action

5 QUALITY SYSTEM LIFE-CYCLE ACTIVITIES
    5.1   General
    5.2   Contract review
    5.3   Purchaser's requirements specification
    5.4   Development planning
    5.5   Quality planning
    5.6   Design and implementation
    5.7   Testing and validation
    5.8   Acceptance
    5.9   Replication, delivery and installation
    5.10 Maintenance

6 QUALITY SYSTEM SUPPORTING ACTIVITIES (not phase dependent)
    6.1   Configuration management
    6.2   Document control
    6.3   Quality records
    6.4   Measurements
    6.5   Rules, practices and conventions
    6.6   Tools and techniques
    6.7   Purchasing

6.8   Included software product

6.9   Training

Some of these paragraphs you will recognize from ISO 9001, while others are completely new. To simplify things, ISO 9000-3 contains a cross-reference to ISO 9001.

Sometimes I meet software engineers who are frustrated with ISO 9001 and 9000-3. "They do not tell us how to develop quality software," they quite rightly complain. It is important to notice, though, that ISO 9001 (and thus ISO 9000-3) was never intended as a help for the *developers*! The standard is aimed solely at being a tool for the customer. Basically, ISO 9001 makes the supplier implement basic management of software development, and the standard then enforces visibility, so that the customer can see what the developers are doing and judge it. In practice, ISO 9001 and 9000-3 can be used as guides for the supplier's management, helping them to control development and gain insight into what is really going on.

2.3 THE TICKIT INITIATIVE

2.3.1 BACKGROUND

By the end of the '80s, the ISO 9000 standards had become quite popular in Europe. Manufacturers were certified to the ISO 9000 standards in increasing numbers. Some of the certified companies had considerable computer departments developing and maintaining software for internal use, and the certification of these departments varied depending on the auditors' competence and the attitude of the certification body. About this time, companies with software as part of their products started to apply for certification, and soon pure software houses joined in.

Industry in Europe was becoming increasingly apprehensive about ISO 9001 certification of software development and maintenance. It was feared that different certificates might have very different values, thereby removing the rationale for certification. The British software industry, together with the British Department of Trade and Industry, launched an initiative to amend the situation and called it TickIT. The name is constructed from the word "tick" ("check" in America) and "IT" for "Information Technology." The goal was to establish effective and unified certification of software development and maintenance.

The TickIT initiative has been quite successful, and TickIT certificates can be found in many countries in Europe, America, and Asia.

2.3.2 WHAT IS TICKIT?

TickIT is a system for certifying software development organizations to ISO 9001. TickIT comprises six items:

- An interpretation of ISO 9001 for software

- A standard set of requirements on the competence and behavior of certification auditors

- A standardized training course for certification auditors

- A registration scheme for approved certification auditors

- A system for accrediting certification bodies for conducting TickIT certifications

- A logotype to be used on certificates to show TickIT certification

Most of this is documented in the TickIT Guide published by the TickIT initiative.

The TickIT scheme is implemented in Britain and is now handled by the DISC TickIT Office. Today, the British NACCB (National Accreditation Council for Certification Bodies) is the only national accreditation authority issuing TickIT accreditation to certification bodies. This means that in Sweden, for example, all TickIT certification is done under the accreditation of NACCB. This works fine, since most certification bodies operating in Sweden are accredited by NACCB as well as by SWEDAC (Swedish Board for Technical Accreditation), and those authorities recognize each other's accreditations.

RAB (the Registrar Accreditation Board), the U.S. accreditation authority, does not currently support a software-specific scheme for ISO 9001 certification. However, several certification bodies operating in the U.S. are accredited in Britain to conduct TickIT certification. American companies can thus receive TickIT certificates under British accreditation.

 ### 2.3.3 THE TICKIT GUIDE

The TickIT guide is named "Guide to Software Quality Management System Construction and Certification using ISO 9001/EN 29001/BS 5750 Part 1 (1987)." It consists of eight different parts, which come from different places and do not always fit perfectly together. However, all parts are written by experienced persons and are well worth reading. This is the table of contents:

Part 1 Introduction
Part 2 The Application of ISO 9001 to Software
Part 3 Purchaser's Guide
Part 4 Supplier's Guide
Part 5 Auditor's Guide
Appendix A TickIT Professional Attributes/
                    Performance Standards for Software
                    Quality Management Auditors
Appendix B Quality Assessment Guides Subsumed
                    into TickIT
Appendix C Standards Information, Guidance
                    Reading Material and Recommended
                    Reading

Notice that Part 2 is the text of ISO 9000-3 included verbatim.

The TickIT Guide can be ordered from:

DISC TickIT Office
389 Chiswick High Road
LONDON W4 4AL
Phone: 44 171 602 8536
Fax: 44 171 602 8912

2.3.4 TICKIT AUDITORS

What's really special about TickIT certification is the auditors. TickIT auditors are registered by the International Register of Certificated Auditors (IRCA) in London. TickIT auditors come in three levels: "Provisional TickIT Auditor," "Senior TickIT Auditor," and "Lead TickIT Auditor." In order to become one, you have to fulfill several requirements:

- You must yourself have worked for at least three years in software development, including all different types of work.

- You must have successfully concluded an approved one-week TickIT auditor's course ending with a formal examination.

- You must have experience as a manager.

- To become Senior or Lead TickIT auditor, you must have experience in conducting and leading, respectively, TickIT certifications.

- There are further requirements regarding your personal attributes.

IRCA shows all signs of taking the requirements for TickIT auditors seriously. In 1993, it was reported that 15% of the applicants for registration as TickIT auditors were not called for an interview, and of those interviewed, 25% failed.

2.3.5 TICKIT CERTIFICATION

All this means that when you apply for TickIT certification, you know that your software development and maintenance procedures will be judged by well trained auditors with personal experience in software development. To assess a software development quality system is, to a degree, a question of judgment. TickIT auditors are taught not to be insistent on literal fulfillment of all requirements in ISO 9001. Instead, they are encouraged to use their own professional judgment to ascertain whether activities are under control. If so, they are accepted, even though the control may not be exactly as prescribed by the standard. This indicates that there is a certain element of subjectivity in TickIT audits (as in most other types of auditing). However, the TickIT Guide and the standardized training of TickIT auditors still give a comprehensive framework.

TickIT certifications are conducted in the same manner as other certifications to ISO 9001. However, ISO 9000-3 is included in the TickIT Guide, and TickIT auditing is done to ISO 9000-3. However, nonconformances are raised to ISO 9001.

2.4 WHY COMPLY WITH ISO 9001?

Is it necessary to fulfill the requirements in ISO 9001 in order to be able to supply quality software products? Definitely not; small organizations, especially, may well be able to produce quality products without going into all the paraphernalia of ISO 9001. However, they will probably only be able to demonstrate their capability by referring to earlier projects.

One reason for a company to implement a quality system in accordance with ISO 9001 is, of course, when this is a contract requirement. Some customers require visible control of the supplier's operation as well as comprehensive records of what has been done. However, I have met several software development managers who apply the requirements in ISO 9001 even though there is no external pressure to do this. "We need to do something about the way we manage and work," goes the usual reasoning, "so why not use ISO 9001 as a tool?" Of course, the choice of ISO 9001 is made with an eye on the possibility that customers will require compliance later.

I noted that *certification* to ISO 9000 standards is becoming popular. Why would a software company take pains to get a third-party certificate of its conformance to ISO 9001?

The reason that first comes to mind, of course, is that a certificate has value in the customers' eyes. The certificate says something about the supplier's capability for delivery of quality products, and holding an ISO 9000 certificate is therefore often used in marketing. Also, in some contract proposal procedures today, you are not welcome to bid if your company does not hold an appropriate ISO 9000 certificate.

The second reason for acquiring a certificate is the need to improve a company's ability, irrespective of customers' views on certification. The certificate is used as a target for the improvement of the company's management, procedures, and so on, with the certification by external auditors as a combined stick and carrot.

INTERPRETING THE REQUIREMENTS IN ISO 9001 FOR SOFTWARE DEVELOPMENT AND MAINTENANCE

3.1 GENERAL

Now, let's take a detailed look at the requirements in ISO 9001 from the viewpoint of a company developing software.

Remember that the standard was originally intended for the manufacturing industry, and its application to software development is a special case. In this section, the requirements are interpreted for software development approximately in accordance with ISO 9000-3 and the TickIT guide.

The requirements in the standard are structured into 20 main *elements*. These elements are seen as the major parts of a quality system, and each element is a well-known concept in the quality management community. In this chapter, we will go through the quality elements in turn and describe what they imply for the development and maintenance of software. In the heading for each quality element we include the corresponding ISO 9001 paragraph number in brackets.

Especially with software, when an auditor encounters a deficiency, there may be more than one paragraph in the standard against which to raise the nonconformance. For example, improper documentation of testing may be raised against either 4.5, "Document control," 4.4.8, "Design validation," or 4.10, "Inspection and testing."

3.2 QUALITY ELEMENTS OF ISO 9001

3.2.1 MANAGEMENT RESPONSIBILITY (4.1)

This element covers the general responsibilities of a company's management. The requirements consist of three parts: quality policy, organization, and management review.

3.2.1.1 Quality Policy

The concept of *quality policy* is central to ISO 9001. The quality policy is viewed as the root from which the rest of the quality system grows.

The standard does not explicitly require a supplier to produce quality products. Instead, the standard requires the supplier management to issue a *quality policy,* where it says that the company shall produce quality products.

Notice that not all suppliers have product quality as an important aim. Quality is important mainly when one wants the customers to return. For example, there are organizations whose only goal is to sell products or services regardless of the needs of the customer or even the quality of the product. Such organizations cannot meet ISO 9001.

The quality policy shall:

- Define the management's commitment to quality

- Define the company's objectives regarding quality, that is, what management *means* by "quality"

- Be relevant to the customer's needs

- Be understood in the organization

- Be implemented

The usual reasons to raise nonconformances regarding quality policy are either that the statement is too vague or the policy is not understood by some staff. Employees in the company do not have to know the quality policy by heart, but they are expected to know the gist of it.

More serious nonconformances have to do with the implementation of the policy. This requirement in the standard forms a kind of "general clause" which can be used to raise nonconformances on slackness in different parts of the company's operation. For example, I once audited a company where I could see that the number of unresolved customer complaints had been increasing for some time because the management had not assigned enough resources to the resolution of customer complaints.

However, the company's quality policy said clearly that meeting the customers' needs was central to the company. Thus, the company did not conform to its own quality policy, and a nonconformance was duly raised. Such a nonconformance should *not* be taken lightly!

Quality policies may be formulated in many different ways. The following is one example:

"XYZ Software Inc. bases its commercial success on the production of quality products and services for its customers. By quality we mean timely delivery of reliable software, prompt response and action on customer complaints, and fulfillment of other customer needs.

"We achieve quality through motivated and skilled staff, defined work procedures, and intensive review and testing activities.

"Each employee is responsible for the quality of his or her work result."

3.2.1.2 Organization

I once audited part of a very large European company, and it was interesting to see that although this company is formalistic in most of its operations, software development was not. The software engineers were apparently experienced and competent, and they worked together in an informal way. No real project managers were appointed; the more senior software engineers fixed it among themselves. Who should do the testing was agreed to on the spur of the moment when the need arose. Projects were largely left on their own by the line management. I saw no indication that the software produced was of inferior quality, but the handling of software development was still not up to ISO 9001.

The most important and difficult part of the paragraph on organization has to do with *responsibility and authority.* Traditionally in the software community, we have tended to use informal organization with vague assignments of responsibility and, especially, authority. This is not acceptable if we claim fulfillment of ISO 9001.

The standard requires documentation of responsibility, authority and interrelation of all personnel affecting quality. Since virtually all staff in a software organization can influence product quality, this means that if a person has a responsibility or an authority, it must be formally assigned.

If a person has a responsibility, it shall be formally assigned by the appropriate manager. The person shall also have enough authority to fulfill his or her responsibility. The authority shall be formally issued.

Sometimes the concept of "responsibility" creates some confusion. In the context of ISO 9001, responsibility means *a duty to act on one's own accord when something has to be done without being told.* To do what somebody else tells you to do is not a responsibility. Usually, the view is that managers and other key positions have responsibilities, while individual software engineers do as they are told, and as company and project rules prescribe.

Something I would like to have seen in the European company mentioned above was formal assignment of responsibility and authority to line managers, project managers, testers, review leaders, software librarians and others.

The existence of a responsibility that cannot be fulfilled is a nonconformance to ISO 9001. For example, I have found project managers with the clearly stated responsibility to meet a time schedule. However, when asked they have admitted that they don't have the authority to direct the work of project members.

As mentioned, interrelations shall also be defined and documented. This is a popular area for auditors to dig into. Especially interesting are the interrelations between project managers and line managers. Who decides what, how is reporting done, how is approval and control defined? Areas where an auditor would expect to find interfaces defined include:

- Project–line
- Project–customer
- Project–maintenance organization
- Software development–hardware development
- Maintenance organization–help desk
- Sales–development

The standard covers two more areas under the heading "Organization," namely, resources and management representative.

The first area requires that the supplier identify the requirements for resources, provide adequate resources, and assign trained personnel.

The second area requires the appointment of a management representative with authority and responsibility to:

- Ensure that the company fulfills the requirements in ISO 9001

- Report the performance of the quality system to company management

Usually, the quality manager is this management representative.

3.2.1.3 Management Review

This paragraph says that the supplier's management shall periodically review the suitability and effectiveness of the quality system. This is often done by having the quality manager annually present the results of quality audits, statistics of customer complaints, records of corrective actions, and other relevant material at a recorded management meeting. The documentation of this meeting should note who attended, what was presented, what decisions were taken made, and so forth.

3.2.2 QUALITY SYSTEM (4.2)

According to ISO, a *quality system* comprises "the organizational structure, responsibilities, procedures, processes and resources for implementing quality management."

Paragraph 4.2 requires that the supplier's quality system be *documented and implemented*. Procedures, rules, decisions, and so on that are needed to fulfill ISO 9001 shall be put in writing. Existing procedures, rules and so on shall be adhered to.

Notice that this last requirement may be a trap for overzealous organizations. If you have a rule or procedure that is not required by ISO 9001, the standard still requires that it be adhered to.

The paragraph further requires that the outline structure of the documentation covering the quality system be defined in a quality manual, which shall contain or reference the documentation of the quality system.

This paragraph in the standard also includes requirements for quality plans. We cover quality plans later in this chapter.

A typical use of this paragraph of the standard is illustrated by the following example. I was a member of a group auditing a large organization. We found a number of minor nonconformances, which the audited organization corrected at once. For example, we found people using nonapproved design documents, a lack of written procedures for minor activities, and so forth. At the conclusion of the audit, there were no nonconformances open; they had all been closed during the audit. However, we still raised a nonconformance against paragraph 4.2 in the standard. An audit is a sampling, and we had just made spotchecks. Since we had found so many minor nonconformances through spot-checking, we were convinced that there were further shortcomings to be found. So we raised a nonconformance on general weakness of the quality system, and required the auditee to make a thorough review of it.

Other typical nonconformances against 4.2 in ISO 9001 are the existence of written procedures that are not adhered to, as well as suitable development processes that are not documented.

3.2.3 CONTRACT REVIEW (4.3)

Many years ago, I was appointed project manager of a very large project. I was given limits on calendar time and staffing, and I planned and calculated how the project should achieve the software our sales department had promised the customer. All limits were absolute, since the price and delivery date had already been agreed on with the customer. When my planning was finished, I put on a tie and went to present my plan to the company management in our boardroom. I showed a few viewgraphs with time schedules, activities, and manning. The presentation went quite smoothly, and I even received one or two approving grunts from the managing director. Then I put on my last slide, and I still vividly remember the sudden drop in temperature in the room. The slide said: "This is why it is not possible" and listed a few reasons. There were no reserves. There were large holes in the staffing. The calendar time was too short to man the project. The requirements were incomplete and unstable. We would be using new concepts with which we had no experience. I had planned too little time for reviews.

The atmosphere in the room became cold and uncomfortable. The expected barrage started: "Are you really sure that it's impossible?" "I think you have been overly conservative in your estimates." "This is a critical project for our company. We may lose the customer if we don't deliver on time." Inexperienced though I was, I did not buckle, but held to my conclusion that the task *was* impossible. The project was started anyhow with another project manager, and after two years and about $20 million, it was cancelled. Of course, it may feel good to say "I told you so!" but I still feel that the debacle was unnecessary.

In my experience, many of the problems with software projects stem from overselling. The sales department has agreed with the customer about a time schedule and/or a price that the development department cannot achieve. The developers' failure to meet the contract is then assumed to reflect on their ability to handle software projects, while in fact the task was impossible from the beginning.

More recently I observed another example of the same phenomenon. I was auditing a large organization developing software. I happened on the minutes from a decision meeting for a development project. In the minutes, the project manager was reported as saying, "We can only meet the delivery date if everything goes right with the project." The minutes then showed that the meeting (of managers) had decided to go forward without changing the delivery date. I checked up on the project, and it was already late. It was clear that it could not meet the delivery date. I said to one of the participants of the decision meeting, "All of you in that meeting were experienced people. You all must have realized that the project manager said 'It is impossible.' No software project goes without problems." She could give me no explanation at all of the decision. A piquant detail is that this very manager had complained to me previously about the impossible time schedules imposed by the sales department. In this case, I raised a nonconformance against 4.3, "Contract review," because the review had not ensured that the delivery date requirement could be met.

The paragraph in ISO 9001 about "Contract review" is intended to ensure that the supplier checks before contract that the organization will be able to perform what is required by the contract. This shall be done by having those responsible for the actual work (e.g., the development managers) review the contract or the tender and document their acceptance or objections. Typical examples of what an auditor would ask:

- Are the requirements documented and understood?

- Are acceptance criteria included?

- Have requirements differing from the tender been resolved?

- Can the supplier muster enough resources for the contract?

- Can the supplier muster the competence needed for the contract?

- Can the task be completed in time?

The standard does not require the supplier to have the required resources and competence available at contract review. For example, it would then be difficult to issue several bids, not expecting to win all of them. However, an auditor would expect that contract review covers such contingencies. For example, if the supplier were to win all the contracts, can parts be subcontracted?

The standard requires that there be a documented procedure for contract review, and that such reviews be recorded. Furthermore, the standard requires the supplier to identify how contract amendments are made. An auditor would also expect that in projects the handling of the requirements specification between supplier and customer be defined.

3.2.4 DESIGN CONTROL (4.4)

The quality element "Design control" is important for software development, since so much of software development is design. Basically, the requirements are that the development be planned, controlled, and verified. It is a remarkably common failure in many software organizations that software development is conducted in an informal way. Some basic sentiments in 4.4 may be summarized in these two statements:

- If something is not planned, there is no reason to expect it to happen.

- If you do not specify what is to be achieved, there is no reason to expect it to be achieved.

The following are subclauses of paragraph 4.4 in the standard.

3.2.4.1 General

This is a cover clause, which says that the supplier should have and use documented procedures to control and verify the design, so that the requirements are met. ISO 9001 requires that you plan before doing and specify before designing.

General slackness in the design work could be noted by an auditor through reference to this paragraph.

An auditor would expect to find procedures and standards for design, coding, and testing. However, the level of detail in standards may differ considerably between organizations. Also, there is a trade-off between standards and reviewing. For example, I sometimes find detailed rules about how to structure source code. Sometimes one might get a better result by having more general rules, and then check on understandability and modifiability during reviews of the code.

3.2.4.2 Design and Development Planning

The supplier is required to plan design and development activities. In this context, a time schedule does not constitute anything close to a plan. ISO 9000-3 refers to two plans: a *development plan* and a *quality plan.*

A development plan should contain the following:

- A definition of the process or methodology to be used in progressing from the purchaser's requirements to a software product.

- Description of the organization and management of the project; the time schedule, responsibilities, work assignments, and progress control should be covered.

- Description of the phases, work packages or any other units the supplier will divide the project into. This should include input, output, and verification of output. An auditor would probably not accept a development process in which significant intermediate work products were not subject to testing and/or review.

- Description of methods and tools to be used in development.

The quality plan covers acceptance criteria, reviews, tests, configuration management, change control, and error handling. The quality plan should contain:

- Quality targets

- Criteria for the acceptability of input to and output from phases, work packages, and so on

- Identification and planning of the tests and reviews and other verification and validation activities in the project

- Specific responsibilities for quality activities

Neither the development plan nor the quality plan have to *contain* all that information. In practice, such plans usually refer to existing procedures and internal standards.

The concept of a quality plan comes from the manufacturing industry where production is an ongoing activity, for example, with steel entered in one end of a production line, and bolts and nuts coming out in the other end, day after day. The production line activities do not need a specific plan, but quality assurance needs one. Thus, there will be a quality plan prescribing quality activities such as sampling, audits, and so on.

Software development, however, is run in projects that need planning anyway. Therefore, at least for small software projects, there is often no specific quality plan. A "software development plan" or "project plan" covers all activities in the project, including the specific quality assurance activities.

The development and quality plans are important from the point of view of the quality system. If an organization makes detailed prescriptions for software development in a common set of procedures, there will probably be projects for which the procedures should be modified. Other organizations have common procedures only at a high level, and require that the detailed procedures be decided on for each project. In both cases, the project plan is where to describe (or reference) the project-specific procedures. When the plans are approved by whoever is the internal "owner" of the project, the specific quality system modifications and additions for the project are also approved.

Now an interesting question usually pops up: Can we have a very brief company quality system, which only says that the project teams will choose their own way of working and managing quality? Yes we can, if we only want a specific project to fulfill ISO 9001. No we can't, if we want the company quality system to fulfill ISO 9001. When a company is certified to ISO 9001, the certificate is not about a specific project, but about the company as a whole.

3.2.4.3 Organizational and Technical Interfaces

If the design work is done by more than one group, the standard requires that the organizational and technical interfaces between them be identified, documented, and transmitted to those needing the information. To ensure that the interface documentation is kept up to date as the design progresses, the interface documentation shall be reviewed regularly.

The development plan is a good place to describe interfaces between groups. Most larger software projects have milestone meetings when finishing project phases. Usually, the development plan is reviewed at such meetings, and then this specific requirement in the standard is met.

3.2.4.4 Design Input

In software development, one type of design input is some kind of requirements specification. This may be either furnished by the purchaser or prepared by the supplier based on the contract requirements and, when applicable, laws and other "statutory and regulatory requirements." Another kind of design input is design documents used as input to coding.

The requirement in the standard is basically that the requirements and design be documented and under formal change control before they are used as input to any activity. This will be a significant change in how many software organizations operate; this kind of strict formalization often seems unnecessary. The background, of course, is that the standard wants to ensure that the work product of each step meets what is required of it. To ensure this, one must be sure that all changes in the basis for the work will be included in the result. "But it works very well for us without having specifications under early change control," you may say. Fine; by all means, continue that way if you want. But don't seek ISO 9001 certification. For that, your organization needs to be able to convince an external auditor that your way of working will continue to work okay. (See Section 4.4 for a discussion of prototyping, though.)

However, some software organizations try to squeeze calendar time by doing as much work as possible in parallel. This tends to lead to project members using preliminary versions of specifications as the basis for their work. Formally, this is a nonconformance with the standard, but a competent auditor will accept such a procedure if he or she can see that the work result will eventually be in accordance with the final version of the specification. For example, there might be a specific review of the final work result to ensure that it meets the final version of the specification.

Paragraph 4.3.3 in the standard requires that there be a procedure for contract amendments. In software development, requirement changes are common, so there must be a procedure for handling new and changed requirements from the purchaser.

3.2.4.5 Design Output

In software development, design output is both the design documentation and the source code. The standard requires that the design documents and the source code be reviewed before release for subsequent use.

There shall be a process for acceptance of the design output, and the criteria for acceptance shall be defined. This is not as complicated as it looks. For example, the review might be the process for acceptance, and the criterion would be acceptance by the review team.

3.2.4.6 Design Review

Formal, documented technical reviews of design results shall be planned and conducted. The review team shall include sufficient competence. The project functions (e.g., coding and testing) for which the result under review is important shall be represented at the review.

This is an area where I have noted many nonconformances. Software engineers say, "But we *do* review everything. It's only that our reviews are informal. Do we really have to plan them and write minutes of meetings? That would not make our reviews more efficient." But it would. In the long run, informal reviews deteriorate. With tight pressure on time, personal disagreements, and all other disturbances, informal reviewing soon becomes sporadic and inefficient. This is not to say that there should not be informal reviews. Colleagues helping each other by reading each other's work results is a very good way to work. However, in order to rely on reviews, both the supplier management and the customers as well as possibly a certification body must *see* that the reviews take place and what they achieve.

Once while auditing a company I began to suspect that their reviewing activities were just formalities, which found only simple formal errors. I then had a look at the documentation of errors found in system testing. I picked one error and asked, "Why was this error not found in a review?" The supplier's representatives hummed a bit, but at last they agreed that they would have to do something about their reviewing. In this way, it is possible to find out if the reviewing works; but the auditor would still need documentation of the reviews.

A common method of ensuring that reviews actually look into what they should is to issue checklists to be used by reviewers. The checklists remind the reviewers what they should give special attention to, but the checklists have another important function. If the checklists used are included in the review report, it is possible afterwards to see what the review checked. Usually, when something should be improved in software development, one part of the improvement is the addition of further points to some checklist.

Examples of nonconformances with this part of the standard include:

- No procedure for formal reviews

- No follow-up of correction of errors found in reviews.

3.2.4.7 Design Verification

The design documentation and the code shall, at appropriate stages, be subject to reviews and/or tests to verify that they meet the requirements. Paragraph 4.10, "Inspection and testing," in ISO 9001 is also about testing, but it is usually used regarding final testing only.

Design verification usually consists of reviews (see above), module testing, and integration testing. Sometimes, developers want to keep verification informal. "Errors are caught in system testing anyhow," they say. Forget it. If your quality policy says that your ambition is to produce quality products, you have to use all available means to catch design errors.

3.2.4.8 Design Validation

The supplier shall conduct a specific activity to ensure that the final software product conforms to requirements. Normally, this activity is a final system test of the complete software product. However, reviewing may also be included, for example, of user documentation. This is an overlap with paragraph 4.10, "Inspection and testing."

Validation shall be a planned and documented process. Sometimes, it is up to the individual tester how to test and what to do about errors. I recently visited a supplier of control systems for cars. Very often, their testing consisted of an employee borrowing a car for the weekend. When driving, he or she was then required to note all disturbances. It is possible that in specific cases this would be the appropriate way to test, but then an auditor would expect to find this decision explicitly made and documented.

"Our testing is sufficient. If something is wrong, the customers will notice it in their own testing." This is the wrong thing to say to an ISO 9001 auditor. The supplier is assumed to be responsible for product quality. However, customers sometimes explicitly take on the task of helping the supplier with beta testing. This cannot be faulted by an ISO 9001 auditor, as long as the beta testing is covered by a clear agreement between the supplier and the beta-testing customer.

3.2.4.9 Design Changes

There are usually a lot of changes to specifications and code, during both initial development and the maintenance phase. Since software is so complex, changes may be dangerous for the following reasons:

- The introduced modification may not lead to the required change in the product.

- Changes often introduce errors in the software.

- A modification of the software may disrupt the "architecture" of the software, thus making later modifications more difficult and error-prone.

- There is a risk of specifications and code diverging because of changes in one but not the other. After a while, specifications may be of no use for further modifications. Of course, the source code is sometimes expected to diverge from some early documents. Such documents can be viewed as tools for thought during the project, and when finished they have value as reference material only. The documentation actually maintained may differ between development models; an auditor will make a judgment as to whether sufficient documentation is under change control.

This means anyone trying to judge the software development process of a supplier will definitely want to see that modification activities are properly controlled.

ISO 9001 requires that after the release of a design document or a source program, all changes of it shall be through a formal process whereby the changes are documented, reviewed, and approved before implementation.

The standard does not explicitly say when a document or program shall be released. Some suppliers try to avoid a cumbersome change process by saying that requirements and design documents will not be released until some point late in the project (e.g., after final testing). Thus, they think if, for example, a programmer finds an error in the design document he or she is using as input, anyone can correct the error immediately without much ado.

However, uncontrolled changes to complex technical documents or programs are extremely dangerous, and, as we saw in 3.2.4.4, the standard does not allow it. Modifications and error corrections are tricky and dangerous operations, so ISO 9001 requires a formal, cumbersome modification procedure just in order to slow the process down and ensure that it is handled correctly.

3.2.5 DOCUMENT AND DATA CONTROL (4.5)

For us, "documents and data" mean information that in some way controls the development or maintenance of software. Examples of such documents are:

- Requirements specifications

- Design documents

- Plans

- Source code files

- Work procedures

- Internal and external standards

Briefly, the standard requires that those who need some document or some data shall have access to it, and they shall be using the appropriate version. Changes to documents and data shall be controlled.

3.2.5.1 General

The supplier shall use documented procedures to control documents and data. External documents such as customer documents, contracts, and programming language manuals shall also be under control. Both documents and data can be on any form of media (e.g., hard copy or electronic media).

When auditing against ISO 9001, I frequently raise nonconformance to 4.5, "Document and data control." Typical nonconformances are:

- Someone is using a document that should be approved but is not.

- Somebody uses the wrong version of a specification or a plan.

- I find two documents with the same identity and the same version number, but different contents.

- Someone using a document cannot explain how he or she knows that it is the appropriate version.

- Someone needing a document for his or her work does not have easy access to it.

3.2.5.2 Document and Data Approval and Issue

The documents and data shall be reviewed and approved before issue. For paper originals, this is usually indicated by signatures on the documents. When the original is stored electronically, one might use separate document lists where the appropriate version of a document is signed off to indicate review and approval. There are also cases where "electronic signatures" are used. Document control procedures and/or tools then ensure that signatures are not entered by mistake.

The standard requires the supplier to maintain a document list (or procedure) whereby one can easily find out which is the current version of any document.

The document control procedures shall ensure that pertinent issues of documents are available everywhere they are needed. This is not too difficult, but the next requirement is that the document control procedures shall ensure that all invalid and/or obsolete documents are removed from use or clearly marked.

In a manufacturing industry, there are relatively few documents. If a new version of a procedure or drawing is issued, someone can walk around with the new version and physically withdraw the old version from all places where it is used.

In software development we have many documents, and they frequently change. Still, we need to know that people use the right versions of all documents. A popular way to achieve this in the software industry is to put all procedures, specifications, programs, and so forth on the computer network and have people read them from the screen rather than each having their own paper copy. This works if it is easy enough to find documents and read them on-line. Otherwise, people will print out their own paper copies, and we don't know if they are using the proper version.

Other methods are:

• Distribution lists for all documents, so that all users get the new versions. Users are instructed to destroy or mark the old version.

• Prominent publication of the fact that a document has been changed, combined with a requirement on people to furnish themselves with the new version and destroy or mark the old one.

Whichever method the supplier is using, the important thing is whether it works. When auditing, I usually ask the persons I interview to show me the documents they are using.

3.2.5.3 Document and Data Changes

When a document or some data is changed, it shall be clear who shall review and approve the change. If it is practicable, a description of the change shall be included in the document or prepared as an attachment.

3.2.6 PURCHASING (4.6)

A few years ago, an English company had won a large order for some complex computer-controlled equipment. The contract contained a comprehensive set of requirements on the supplier's software development, including the fulfillment of ISO 9001. In the beginning of the contract, I was employed by the customer to conduct an audit of the supplier to ensure that their plans and processes for software development were okay. I planned to spend two days at the supplier's premises, and I sent them a rough audit program for those days, which they accepted.

Then I arrived, together with the customer's representative, and we met with some of the managers in a conference room. They were very glad to meet us, but they did not have any software development at all. They had subcontracted it to a company in Australia, and their happy faces indicated that they did not have a care in the world.

"So," I said, "but you are still responsible for the quality of the product and the timeliness of your delivery?" "Ye-es," came the answer from a not-so-confident manager. "Well then, will the quality of the software be sufficient and will it be finished on time?" I asked. This time, the affirmative answer was even more hesitating. Then I went in for the kill: "Convince me!" I said.

It took the whole two days. Finally, the supplier's managers realized that when you subcontract software development from a distant subcontractor, you have an even more difficult situation than if you were to develop the software inside your own organization. They had to plan for a number of activities:

- Journeys to Australia to audit the subcontractor's software development

- Their own review of the subcontractor's plans, specifications, and code

- A system for distributing modified requirements to the subcontractor

- Procedures and criteria for acceptance of the software

- Configuration management and maintenance of the software delivered from the subcontractor

Paragraph 4.6 in ISO 9001 specifies requirements on purchasing. A peculiarity with ISO 9001 is that even if a supplier is bound by the contract to fulfill ISO 9001, the ISO 9001 requirements don't have to be imposed on the subcontractors. Instead, paragraph 4.6 in the standard contains requirements on how to control subcontractors. The following describes some of the subparagraphs of 4.6. "Supplier" denotes the organization on which the standard puts requirements. "Subcontractor" is the organization from which the supplier purchases software, hardware, or services.

3.2.6.1 General

As usual, the supplier shall follow documented procedures. It shall be ensured that purchased products conform to requirements. Notice that the requirements in 4.6 are not about the purchase of pencils and erasers, but about parts of the product and tools that may affect product quality. A special case is the purchase of services. Sometimes, suppliers are not clear whether they are hiring consultants to help them with development or purchasing the development of a certain item. If you purchase manpower only, the standard only requires you to follow a procedure for ensuring that you get the right people. The work done by these people will be controlled directly by the supplier, not the subcontractor.

How do we ensure that purchased software conforms to requirements? It depends on the type of software and its importance, but usually some or all of the following are used:

- Contract requirements on the subcontractor's procedures

- Audits of the subcontractor's quality system

- Checking the subcontractor's past performance

- Surveillance of the subcontractor during the contract

- Witnessing reviews and testing

- Test and review of deliverables from the subcontractor

3.2.6.2 Evaluation of Subcontractors

The supplier shall evaluate all subcontractors. This means that someone with the necessary authority and competence shall judge each subcontractor and decide whether to use each one. This decision and its rationale shall be documented.

When using a subcontractor, the supplier shall decide what control is to be exercised over the subcontractor. Notice that the standard does not say how much control to impose. The requirement is that the supplier make a decision based on relevant facts. For a subcontractor developing software, the amount of control may vary, depending, for example, on the subcontractor's past performance and the importance of the subcontracted item. Examples of control options are:

- Regular audits of the subcontractor's quality system and its application

- Review of the subcontractor's plans

- Witnessing the subcontractor's reviews and test

- Supplier approval of individual work results (e.g., plans, specifications, code, or test results) as they are produced by the subcontractor

A special case is when the software is purchased through retail. In this case, the "subcontractor" is the organization with which the purchase is conducted, not the original developer of the software. In such a case, it is formally the retailer's responsibility to control *its* subcontractor. However, sometimes the buyer still requires access to the developing organization in order to be able to evaluate its quality system. Of course, in the case of off-the-shelf software products in extensive use on the market, the need and opportunity for explicit control may be slight. If you are purchasing software through retail, ISO 9001 requires that you define to what extent you put requirements on the retailer to control its supplier.

The supplier shall maintain a list of acceptable subcontractors.

3.2.6.3 Purchasing Data

The items subcontracted or purchased shall be well specified. Requirements on the subcontractor's development process shall be documented in the contract, as shall requirements for the supplier to approve work results and procedures.

Before purchase, the purchasing data shall be reviewed by the supplier.

3.2.6.4 Verification of Purchased Product

The auditor expects to find documentation of a decision about the verification of each purchased development tool or included product. There are several different cases to consider.

- A tool supporting the development or validation of software is purchased. The quality of the tool does not influence the quality of the supplier's product or the quality of the service to the customer. In this case, the decision may be to do no verification.

- A tool or included product is purchased, that is an off-the-shelf item and has been used extensively by other suppliers for some time. Examples are compilers and operating systems. In this case, the decision *may* be to view the item as a "proven design" and do no or little verification. Notice, however, that extensive use of older versions of the tool or included product may be insufficient evidence of "proven design."

- The purchase concerns development and production of some new hardware or software. In this case, a reasonable decision may be to put requirements on the subcontractor's development and production (including testing), and to check that these requirements are fulfilled. Witnessing of the subcontractor's testing and/or the supplier performing specific acceptance testing may be appropriate.

- A tool or included product is purchased, which is already developed and produced but has not been extensively used. An example may be an operating system version for a new type of processor board. In this case, the supplier has to become convinced that this purchased product meets the requirements. In this case the verification may include collection of the experiences of other users, as well as extensive testing.

Examples of common nonconformances with 4.6 include:

- No list of approved suppliers

- Inappropriate control of subcontractor

- No documented verification of purchased items

- Inappropriate contract with subcontractor

3.2.7 CONTROL OF CUSTOMER-SUPPLIED PRODUCT (4.7)

Once I encountered a situation which puzzled me at first. The customer used two suppliers to each deliver one part of the product. Supplier A developed some basic software which was also included in the software developed by supplier B. The software was delivered directly from A to B. The question was: Who was responsible for the functioning of A's software inside B's products? Surprisingly, the answer was: The customer! It was the customer who required B to use software from A, so the formal way to look at the relationship was that the customer first purchased the basic software from A and then delivered it to B. Paragraph 4.7 in ISO 9001 covers such situations, where the customer supplies software to be included in the product.

The standard says that the supplier shall have procedures for verification, storage, and maintenance of customer-supplied software. However, the quality of this software is the responsibility of the customer.

An auditor would expect the supplier to have procedures for identification, version handling, and error reporting for customer-supplied software.

Notice that even if the customer requires two suppliers to cooperate regarding software developed by one and included by the other, the ultimate responsibility lies with the customer. Unclear division of responsibility between customer and supplier is a common nonconformance with this paragraph in the standard.

3.2.8 PRODUCT IDENTIFICATION AND TRACEABILITY (4.8)

This paragraph is used to make the software supplier keep control of such issues as:

- For each software specification, on what preceding document and issue is it based?

- For each source code module and design document, on which specification(s) is it based?

- What error corrections and amendments have been included in which source programs?

- What happened to each problem report? What decisions were made, what changes, what testing, and so forth?

- From what source program versions was a specific load module generated?

The auditor may very well bring up the identity of a certain item and ask a manager, "How do you know that this item is the correct version?" The auditor would not expect the manager to have checked this specific item. Rather, an appropriate answer might be something like: "Our procedure XYZ-123 ensures that all items of this kind have the right version. In our internal audits, we have checked that the procedure is adhered to. If you like, we could go to the development library and trace this item to its requirements."

It is surprising how often I have found deficiencies in this area when auditing. Examples are:

- The wrong version of a source file is in a library

- A change was reported as introduced, but was not.

- A manager or project leader was unable to show what source code versions were used in system test.

- Insufficient traceability of change requests was exhibited.

3.2.9 PROCESS CONTROL (4.9)

This paragraph covers general requirements on the control of production, installation, and servicing. For software, the paragraph is used for requirements on the control of replication and installation. Replication is the process of writing to a diskette, tape, PROM, or other medium, the load module(s) and data to be delivered.

The auditor would expect to find a documented procedure for the replication process in operation. Also, he or she would look for a procedure for the handling of master PROMs or master libraries, to ensure that the correct versions are always used.

Nonconformances raised against this paragraph of the standard frequently include:

- No documented procedure for replication

- Improper handling of master PROMs or diskettes

3.2.10 INSPECTION AND TESTING (4.10)

Since ISO 9001 was written for the manufacturing industry, paragraph 4.10 is aimed at inspection and testing of *produced goods*.

Thus, we use this paragraph for requirements on the inspection and testing done in connection with replication. The auditor expects to find written procedures for the inspection and testing to be done at replication. What makes the supplier confident that the software is replicated correctly and from the correct version of the master software?

It is especially important that there be appropriate procedures in operation if the replication process includes compilation, linking, and/or parameterization.

Nonconformances in this area may be:

- The equipment for programming PROMs also checks on the result. The function of this automatic check has not been regularly inspected.

• There is no documented procedure for testing PROMs.

Inspection and testing during development is covered in ISO 9001 paragraph 4.4.7 under "design verification." Final testing is covered in paragraph 4.4.8 under "design validation." Some auditors may, however, also use paragraph 4.10 in the standard for requirements on final testing of software.

3.2.11 CONTROL OF INSPECTION, MEASURING, AND TEST EQUIPMENT (4.11)

This paragraph mainly covers requirements on the calibration of measuring equipment. In software development, we do not usually have much measuring equipment that needs calibration. Possible examples may be:

• Clocks for testing timing requirements

• Voltmeters for testing programs that operate D/A converters

• Line analyzers

Estimation methods may need calibration. Often, estimations are based on typical values experienced in earlier projects. These values must be checked as time goes by to ensure that they are still appropriate.

The standard requires that the supplier select the appropriate measuring equipment and follow a documented procedure for the control of this equipment. There shall be a list of all instruments needing calibration. The instruments shall be calibrated at prescribed intervals, and they shall be marked with calibration status.

Apart from measuring equipment, paragraph 4.11 in the standard also covers test tools. For example, if you use a test data generator, you have to regularly check that it generates the right test cases. This regular check is required even if your tool is software and does not wear down. Your types of applications and your way of testing may vary and make the testing tool less appropriate. Also, this paragraph in the standard may be used as a requirement that each new version of a software tool for testing be checked for sufficiency.

3.2.12 INSPECTION AND TEST STATUS (4.12)

ISO 9001 requires that specifications and programs be verified, usually through reviews and/or testing. The supplier shall have procedures that preclude the use of unverified specifications or programs.

An auditor will expect to see that:

- It is easy to ascertain whether a certain item has been reviewed, tested, and approved. Usually, this is achieved by the maintenance of a list of specifications and source programs with their current status.

- Unverified specifications and programs are kept apart from verified items (e.g., in a different directory).

A typical nonconformance is when somebody is using a specification and does not know whether it has been approved.

3.2.13 CONTROL OF NONCONFORMING PRODUCT (4.13)

A nonconforming product is a specification or program that either does not fulfill the requirements or has not been developed in accordance with prescribed procedures.

Paragraph 4.13 requires that the supplier have procedures to ensure that nonconforming products not be used unintentionally. For software, this means that the auditor will look for:

- Clear identification of controlled items that contain uncorrected errors. Of course, during the preparation of a document or program, it will be incorrect most of the time. However, it cannot become a nonconforming product until it is in some way "frozen."

- A method to elicit customer acceptance of delivery of nonconforming software, for example, in the case of a prerelease version.

In some cases, there is a need for emergency modification of software. Either the organization operating the software must, for their business, be able to get quick changes every now and then; or perhaps a critical error might pop up in an important computer application. In these cases, there sometimes isn't time to apply the ordinary rigorous development procedures. "Control of nonconforming product" in this case means that:

- An auditor would expect to find a procedure for handling quick modifications.

- The fact that the modified specifications and source programs have not been handled in the normal way must be documented.

- It must be possible to see that afterwards the modified items will always be elevated to the same status as the rest of the software, for example, through specific reviewing.

A nonconformance would be raised against paragraph 4.13 in the standard if it were unclear which documents and programs contained detected errors.

3.2.14 CORRECTIVE AND PREVENTIVE ACTION (4.14)

ISO 9001 is weak on requirements for continuing improvement of the supplier's work processes and product quality. This is perhaps natural, since the standard was originally intended for use in single contracts. If we as customers meet this supplier in only one acquisition, we are not very interested in long-term improvements. Those will only benefit other customers.

However, paragraph 4.14 contains some requirements for "self-sharpening" of the software development process. The paragraph contains requirements on the improvement of products as well.

Basically, the paragraph contains three requirements:

1. The effective handling of customer complaints and other reports indicating that the software product does not conform to requirements

2. The effective handling of audit reports and other information indicating shortcomings in the development process

3. The active collection and analysis of available information about product and process nonconformance, and the proper actions to prevent problems in other software

The first requirement concerns normal correction of errors reported from customers, and this is not difficult to make software developers and managers understand. However, I frequently find it difficult to make software managers understand the implications of the other two. Let me try to explain.

The idea of ISO 9001 paragraph 4.14 is that information about problems encountered should drive improvements of the development process. If a weakness is found in the process, an improvement action shall be taken as soon as possible. When errors are found in the software, aside from the immediate correction of the errors, an analysis of the root causes shall be conducted. If possible, actions shall then be taken to improve the process to prevent recurrence of these specific types of errors.

A common way to handle the root-cause analysis is to have a group of persons meet (for example, every third month) to review all reports from design and code reviews, testing, customer complaints, and quality audits together with complaints and improvement suggestions from the staff. If the group finds that something shall be done, a corrective action is initiated in the same way as corrective actions prompted by quality audits. Then there is regular follow-up of the progress of all corrective actions.

Auditors frequently find serious nonconformances to this paragraph in ISO 9001. A few examples:

- A customer complaint has not been properly handled.

- A deficiency has been found in an internal quality audit, but not corrected.

- There is no procedure to ensure that all problems are analyzed and acted upon.

- There is no procedure for reporting difficulties with applying rules and procedures.

3.2.15 HANDLING, STORAGE, PACKAGING, PRESERVATION, AND DELIVERY (4.15)

This paragraph is about the handling (etc.) of produced goods. Thus, we apply it to software that has been replicated and is sitting in a PROM, a diskette, or another medium. We also use the paragraph for requirements on the handling of finished software that is kept in a repository (e.g., product libraries), either for use as masters when replicating, to be used when modifying the software product, or to be reused in new products.

The supplier shall use procedures for the handling and storage of software media so that damage and deterioration are prevented. For example, magnetic media shall be refreshed at regular intervals. Media shall be labelled and packed appropriately.

Repositories for software (including data and tools) shall be backed up. The repositories shall be protected for unintentional damage (e.g., through access limitations). This last point has to do with our deplorable tendency to do hurried, unauthorized changes.

Even if there is a strict formal process for how to modify software, there is the risk of *spontaneous changes*. Imagine that you are a programmer on a project team. Your program has been reviewed and approved and put under formal change control. The day after the review, you suddenly become aware of an embarrassing minor error in your program. The natural action is to quickly make a simple modification of the program original, without anyone noticing. The risk is, however, that in your haste you botch the modification, or by introducing this change you affect some completely different function in the program without noticing.

To ensure against this type of spontaneous change, an organization should see to it that programs and specifications that are put under formal change control are stored with some access restrictions.

3.2.16 CONTROL OF QUALITY RECORDS (4.16)

When purchasing complex software products to be developed by a supplier, the customer needs confidence in the delivered product. Basically, there are three means for the customer to achieve this confidence:

- Past performance. The customer will check on the supplier's success with previous undertakings.

- The customer's own testing of the software.

- The customer's insight into the supplier's development process.

As software products grow more complex, customers have to rely more on the last alternative. During development and maintenance, the customer will require opportunities to see what is happening. The most important source for information about the effectiveness of the software development process is *quality records*. Quality records are documents which show that actions have been taken to ensure or check quality. Examples of quality records are:

- Minutes from management review (2.1.3)

- Minutes from contract review (2.3)

- Records of reviews of specifications and programs (2.4.6)

- Records of the follow-up of review remarks

- Records of subcontractor evaluations (2.6)

- Records of all reported errors from report to clearance

- Quality audit reports

- Test plans and reports

- Documentation of corrective actions

- Purchasing documentation

The standard requires that there be a procedure for the handling of quality records. The records shall be safely stored and easily accessible. After a specified period following the end of the project, quality records shall be disposed of.

Typical nonconformances are:

- There are no rules for the retention of quality records.

- Review records are not kept.

- Test records are not kept.

- The period for keeping quality records is not defined.

3.2.17 INTERNAL QUALITY AUDITS (4.17)

It is not enough for a certified supplier to be audited regularly by the certification body. The supplier shall also have an independent part of the organization regularly audit all operations that may affect product or service quality.

Such internal quality audits shall investigate:

- Whether the work performed in software development adheres to plans and procedures

- Whether the quality system is *effective* (i.e., that existing procedures, etc. are the right ones)

Internal quality audits are conducted on behalf of company management. The auditor or auditors must be independent of the operation audited; the person auditing a certain department must not be a member of that department, or he or she could not audit the department management.

Often, the audits are planned and managed by the company quality manager, who uses persons from different parts of the company to audit each other's departments.

Since software development is usually conducted in projects, quality audits must go into different projects to check on the usefulness of and adherence to the quality system. Such audits are called "project audits." Other aspects of the company are best audited by focusing on what lies outside projects (e.g., line management, corrective action, and training). Such audits are called "system audits."

All parts of the quality system shall be audited regularly at specified intervals. Some parts may need to be audited more frequently than others due to their importance. There shall be an *audit plan,* which shows what internal audits will be conducted in the near future, usually during the next 12-month period. Quality audits shall be planned and reported, and deficiencies found shall be corrected (see 2.14).

Typical nonconformances are:

- No audit plan

- Audit plan not up to date

3.2.18 TRAINING (4.18)

The standard does not require that the supplier employ good people or excellent technicians. That would not be reasonable or checkable. Instead, the standard requires that the supplier see to it that the staff are trained for their tasks.

Paragraph 4.18 requires the supplier to have a procedure to:

- Identify training needs for each staff position

- Provide such training

- Keep records of the training of all staff members

In Sweden, much of this is covered by procedures for "career reviews" in which managers sit down with each subordinate and go through their work situation, career prospects, and different kinds of needs.

Examples of the kinds of training an auditor would expect to see planned are:

- New programming languages and tools

- Audit training for internal quality auditors

- Project management training

What kind of training should there be? Is it sufficient to let a programmer sit with the manual for the new programming language for a couple of days? Well, it is not really up to the auditors to judge your means of training and education. As long as the training is documented and *sufficient*, the auditor should be satisfied. The criterion for sufficient training is that the person is capable of performing his/her work to a high enough standard. The auditor may see this, for example, in review records and project success. However, quality auditors and other staff who need specific qualifications should be able to produce records of formal training.

Typical nonconformances are:

- No procedure for planning of training

- No training records

- Some employee who has not received proper training for his or her task.

3.2.19 SERVICING (4.19)

The standard says that the supplier shall have documented procedures for servicing *if this is required in the contract.* The standard talks about the repair of delivered items; for example, sending somebody out to repair a faulty refrigerator.

In the software business, this paragraph is about maintenance, that is, error corrections and enhancements to delivered software. Paragraph 4.14, "Corrective and preventive action," requires that the supplier have a way to receive customer complaints. Using paragraph 4.19, the auditor requires the supplier to have procedures for handling complaints and requests for modifications. The supplier can avoid these requirements only if there is no maintenance contract and no warranty commitments.

Since software maintenance is very similar to the initial development on the technical level, most of the requirements in paragraphs 4.4–4.13 apply as well.

A common concern among software suppliers hoping to fulfill ISO 9001 regards the maintenance of old software. Typically, current software development follows a well-defined process with some specific types of documents being produced. These documents do not exist for old software, so the old software cannot be maintained in accordance with the new procedures. The solution is to have specific procedures for maintenance of old software. These procedures might best be documented in the maintenance plans for the different software products. The auditor will only expect to see that the maintenance is under control.

Typical nonconformances are:

• Maintenance work for a customer without a contract

• Specific methods for maintenance of an old product not documented

• No procedure for testing after maintenance activities

3.2.20 STATISTICAL TECHNIQUES (4.20)

Statistical techniques are important when the quality of bolts and nuts is checked through sampling. Paragraph 4.20 is about such checks.

However, for software the paragraph is interpreted as a requirement that the supplier measure the quality of both the products and the development process.

The auditor will look for collection and analysis of data about the number of found errors in different phases, as well as ability to meet deadlines and milestones.

As an auditor I would ask, "How many errors do you find during system test, and how many errors do your customers find for you?" Difficulties in answering that question would lead to a nonconformance.

SOME SPECIFIC ISSUES

4.1   GENERAL

Some specific topics tend to create problems for companies aiming for ISO 9001 certification. In this chapter some of these issues are discussed, although some of them have already been touched on briefly in previous chapters.

In many cases, these discussions arise from cases in which the quality manager is unhappy when trying to make the company's software development conform to the requirements in ISO 9001. A typical lament may be, "I don't know how to handle cases when I myself do not believe in a requirement in the standard. I don't feel sincere trying to enforce the requirement when I believe our software developers actually ought to work in another way." My reaction is always to ask for an example. Up till now, the examples I have been presented with fall into two categories:

1. The requirement is about *records*. Software developers often fail to see the usefulness of preparing and keeping records of reviews, tests, and so on.

2. Literal conformance to the requirement would actually make the company a *less* competent supplier of software.

Regarding category 1, the problem is about understanding and accepting the need for records. This need stems from the fact that an activity must be *auditable* in order to demonstrate conformance to ISO 9001. Also, of course, if an organization is to be able to improve, it has to record what is going on.

Category 2 problems have to do with misunderstandings about the scope and intention of ISO 9001. The TickIT guide, for example, stresses that the auditors shall be careful not to interpret the standard too literally. It isn't a problem if a supplier does not conform to the letter of ISO 9001 as long as what the standard is intended to achieve is accomplished.

4.2 CONCURRENT ENGINEERING

Formally, ISO 9001 requires that a specification be finalized and approved before it is used as the basis for further work. This has been seen as a problem by some companies seeking ISO 9001 certification. These organizations try to shorten the calendar time needed for a project by running activities in parallel as much as possible. They want to do this, for example, by having programmers use specifications before they are finished (i.e., preliminary, nonapproved versions).

The use of preliminary versions of specifications could probably be accepted by a competent auditor, *but only if* he or she can clearly see that the final work result will always conform to the final version of the specification. Also, the auditor would require that records be kept, so that any auditor can see that this has been the case for all projects.

One way to ensure that the final work result (e.g., a program) conforms to the final version of the specification used as its basis is comprehensive reviewing. There should be a strict procedure so that when the specification is approved, the program is thoroughly reviewed and then updated to fulfill the approved version of the specification.

Working to a preliminary specification can sometimes be viewed as *preparation* of the actual work. The programmer does not actually develop a program; he or she just prepares so that when the specification is finally approved, the programming can get a running start. However, if you use this reasoning, you cannot refer to progress in programming until the specification is approved; if the specification work suddenly changes direction, all of your programs may become unsuitable.

4.3 RESEARCH DEPARTMENTS

If your company has long-term research activities going on where software is developed, must the researchers also follow the strict model for software development? Many organizations have "lab" activities, where ideas are tried before decisions are made about development of new products. Such activities frequently pose problems for both the company staff preparing for certification and inexperienced certification auditors, since the researchers usually refuse to follow the general development model for software.

The solution to this problem is to read the title of ISO 9001: "Quality Systems—Model for quality assurance in design, development, production, installation, and servicing." Research is outside the scope of the standard. This means that the detailed requirements about design control, document control, testing, and so forth do not apply to the research department. However, this is only true if the researchers do not develop products. If results from the research (specifications or source code) are used in a product, then we are talking about development, not research.

The fact that the standard does not cover research may not be taken to mean that the research department can be ignored. If the certificate is to cover the whole company, those activities outside the scope of ISO 9001 must also be shown to be under control. The auditor would expect to find documentation of what the researchers are expected to produce, as well as records of reporting and follow-up. If a researcher is completely free to choose his or her line of work, this should be documented.

4.4 PROTOTYPING

4.4.1 PROTOTYPING AS PART OF REQUIREMENTS ANALYSIS

Some requirements are virtually impossible to specify without first trying them out. This is especially true of user interfaces, so developers often create throw-away software in the simplest possible way to try out what the requirements really should look like. The throw-away software is called a *prototype*. It is not developed in accordance with ISO 9001 requirements on design control and so on.

As long as the prototype software is truly throw-away, this is no problem at all. Prototype development is information-gathering, not product development. However, a not-so-uncommon case is when the sales manager happens to find the prototype. "Why, you already have it developed. It just needs some adjustments." Then the sales manager rushes away and promises immediate delivery to a customer. Now you have a problem.

If you sell a prototype, the ISO 9001 auditor will not be happy at all. This would mean that you deliver a product to your customer that is not developed at all in accordance with your quality system, and such behavior is judged very harshly by an auditor.

However, if you take great pains, it might be possible to convince the auditor that before delivery, the prototype is converted into a proper product. I don't know why you'd want to do this, since the conversion would cost more than developing the product fresh, using the information gathered from the prototype. You must have a procedure for this conversion operation, stating how it must be done. This procedure must prescribe that all documents required for a product must be prepared. *Very* comprehensive reviews must be conducted to ensure that the documents are correct.

4.4.2 PROTOTYPING AS A DEVELOPMENT METHOD

Prototyping is sometimes used as a development method, especially in cases where the end users find it difficult to explain what is required of the software. In one organization, the work method was described for me as follows. A requirements specification was written in very general terms at a high level. Thereafter, the programmer would create a program from his or her own head, a prototype. The end user would then try to use the program and come back to the programmer with views on how the final program ought to behave. The programmer would modify the prototype and give it back to the user, who would test it again, and so on. At last, when the user was satisfied with the program, the programmer would write a specification, and the product was finished.

I find it very difficult to imagine how such a development method could be compliant with the design control requirements in ISO 9001. One possible way to look at the method is to see the programmer as a consultant, working in a project under the user's control. Still, it does not help very much.

If this is the way you want to develop software, and if your customers are happy with it, by all means do so, but do not seek ISO 9001 certification. Personally, though, I don't believe in development by prototyping. The result will be a program that has been changed a great number of times, with no requirements and no reviewing of understandability and modifiability. There is no reason to believe that the after-the-fact specification will be accurate or sufficient for maintenance. Development by prototyping is a case of unmanaged software development.

4.5 CONSULTANCY

4.5.1 BACKGROUND

Consultancy companies often want to be software houses, running development projects of their own and taking responsibility for delivering a specific product to their customer. Because of this, they want to be certified to ISO 9001 in order to indicate this capability to prospective customers. A number of complications arise in such cases, and I will discuss them below.

 ### 4.5.2 CONSULTANCY BY SUPPLYING MANPOWER

A company that only supplies manpower to the customers' projects cannot be certified to ISO 9001. Such a company cannot claim to have *design* within its business scope. Its business is only *supply*. The consultants all work under the *customers'* quality systems for design. However, the company might become certified to ISO 9002, which is about "production, installation and servicing." This can create some frustration, since some mistakenly view ISO 9001 as the "highest"-level standard, thus giving certificates higher value. Whether you are certified to ISO 9001, ISO 9002, or ISO 9003 has nothing to do with the "goodness" of your quality system. It only says what kind of operations your company performs. If you do production, ISO 9001 puts exactly the same requirements on your production process as does ISO 9002.

However, if the company were supplying some specific *services*, for example, "Prestudies of the need for computer support in banking," it might be possible to achieve certification to ISO 9001. According to ISO 9001, a service is a product. If the company designs and produces services, it might be able to show conformance to the requirements in ISO 9001 (e.g., regarding design control). Still, such a certificate would not indicate that the company's ability to design and produce *software* has been certified. Each ISO 9001 certificate includes a text about its *scope*, that is, what business areas and activities the certificate covers.

4.5.3 USING THE CUSTOMER'S QUALITY SYSTEM

The fact that a consultancy company uses the customer's quality systems does not in itself preclude certification to ISO 9001. The standard does not require that a company itself invent its entire quality system. The company may even have several different quality systems to use for different kinds of projects. If a company only uses the quality systems of its customers, the following conditions ought to be fulfilled in order for the company to achieve ISO 9001 certification:

- The company shall itself take reponsibility for development projects, and this shall be clear in the contract with the customer.

- The parts of the customer quality system that apply to the company shall be clearly stated in the contract.

- The rest of the quality system needed for the company must exist, be in operation, and fulfill ISO 9001.

- The internal quality audits of the company shall cover all activities conducted under the customer's quality system.

- The internal quality audits of the company shall cover all parts of the customer's quality system used by the company.

- There shall be a mechanism for the company to require and achieve corrective actions regarding those parts of the customer's quality system used by the company.

- In all cases when the company uses a customer's quality system, this shall fulfill the requirements of ISO 9001. This shall be clearly stated in the contract with the customer.

4.5.4 MIXTURES OF CONSULTANCY AND DEVELOPMENT

Some companies do their business in both pure consultancy and development. In order to become certified to ISO 9001, they have to show that both the supply of consultants and the development are under proper control and meet ISO 9001 requirements.

Let's say that one such company has received a certificate to ISO 9001, which covers consultancy as well as development of software. Let us further assume that this company supplies a customer with a project manager for a software development project. The project manager is a consultant and works in accordance with the customer's quality system, which is almost nonexistent. Because of this lack of a proper quality system, the project fails in a spectacular way, and the customer complains in the trade press: "The project was a failure because of our consultant project manager from XYZ-soft. And these guys have been certified to ISO 9001 by QPL-cert Inc.!"

This situation could be extremely damaging for the certification body in question. By issuing the certificate, QPL-cert has vouched for the capability of XYZ-soft, and for a certification body its reputation is its main asset. For this reason, if you want to have both development and consultancy in the scope of your certificate, the certification body will probably require you to undertake consultancy only in cases where a proper quality system is in operation. How this requirement should be formulated may be a matter of debate, but it does not seem reasonable to require you to do consultancy only for customers holding an ISO 9001 certificate.

4.6 OLD SOFTWARE PRODUCTS

Often, a supplier will introduce a number of new rules and standards for software development as a part of the process of achieving compliance with ISO 9001. Usually, the supplier maintains a considerable amount of old software, which was developed according to earlier (or no) rules. Sometimes the maintenance and enhancement of old software is a major part of the supplier's business.

I sometimes get the question, "Do we have to rewrite all the old software to fit our new rules and standard?" Fortunately, the answer is no. Otherwise, ISO 9001 would be unachievable for a large part of the software industry. However, in order to meet ISO 9001, the supplier must show that the maintenance of old software is under proper control.

Proper control might, for example, be a documented procedure for enhancement and error correction in old software. This procedure would identify the following:

- What software products are covered by the procedure

- Responsibilities and authorities regarding this maintenance

- A procedure for error reporting and change requests

- A procedure for configuration management for the old software

- Rules regarding documentation of changes in old software

- Rules regarding review and testing of changed software

Of course, some of the procedures and/or rules identified in the procedure for maintenance of old software may be the same used for new software.

4.7 CUSTOMER TRAINING

Customer training is an important part of some software businesses. In the context of ISO 9001, this is a service, and a service is a kind of product. How to apply the requirements of the standard to a large extent depends on the specific type of customer training undertaken. An auditor would expect to find the following:

- Documented responsibilities and authorities for the development of courses and course material

- Procedures for development and maintenance of courses

- Procedures for configuration management of course material

- Agreements with customers which clearly describe the training to be delivered

- A method for obtaining feedback on customer satisfaction with the training

ISO 9004-2 gives further advice on quality systems for services.

COMPARISONS WITH OTHER SCHEMES

5.1 THE SEI CAPABILITY MATURITY MODEL (CMM)

CMM was developed at the Software Engineering Institute in Pittsburgh, and it is very much a rival to ISO 9001 for software.

CMM is a scheme to classify a software development organization according to its capability. CMM identifies five different maturity levels for software developing organizations. The levels are as follows:

1. Initial: The software development is run informally, and depends on the competence of some persons.

2. Repeatable: There is a common system for project management and control.

3. Defined: There is a common system for the software engineering activities.

4. Managed: The software development process is stable and gives a consistent product quality. Measurements are used to keep the process and product under control.

5. Optimizing: The software development process contains its own improvement process.

There are four main differences between ISO 9001 and CMM:

- ISO 9001 is intended for most industry, while CMM is software-specific.

- CMM is more detailed and specific.

- ISO 9001 establishes one acceptable level of a supplier's management and processes, while CMM is a tool for assessing the supplier's software ability on a scale from one to five.

- ISO 9001 focuses on a customer-supplier relation; CMM is mainly concerned with the software development process as such.

Several papers have been published in recent years discussing the relation between ISO 9001 and CMM (see references). It appears that an organization certified to ISO 9001 would achieve most requirements for CMM level 2, and an organization on CMM level 2 would fulfill most requirements in ISO 9001. There are some requirements in ISO 9001 that are not well covered at any level of CMM. For example, the requirements in ISO 9001 that refer to a *customer* (e.g., 4.3, "Contract review," and the part in 4.14, "Corrective and preventive action," about customer complaints) are not very well covered in CMM, since customers are not conspicuous in CMM's perspective.

Should a software company go for ISO 9001 or CMM? To go for CMM level 2 would be easier in some respects, since CMM is software-specific. The company could also later go for higher levels of productivity and quality. The advantage of ISO 9001 is that the standard is very well known and accepted in different industry branches around the world. A certificate to ISO 9001 is probably more useful than a certificate to a certain CMM level.

The first criterion for choosing between ISO 9001 and CMM is, of course, the need. If you need CMM, for example, to be able to do business with the U.S. Department of Defense (DoD), go for CMM; if, on the other hand, you need an ISO 9001 certificate to do international business, go for that. However, if both are needed, or if there is not a specific need for a documented CMM level, I would recommend that a software organization first go for certification to ISO 9001 according to TickIT, and thereafter use CMM to improve further.

5.2   IEEE 730

The IEEE (Institute of Electrical and Electronics Engineers) publishes a number of software engineering standards. IEEE 730 is titled "IEEE Standard for Software Quality Assurance Plans" and was last revised in 1989. As the title implies, the standard is about a software quality plan. When stating the requirements for the contents of the plan, the standard also puts requirements for the management of software development. IEEE 730 states minimum requirements on the documentation to be produced, and the reviews and audits to be held. "Audit" in this context is something different from the "quality audit" discussed in this book.

IEEE 730 approximately covers paragraph 4.4, "Design control," in ISO 9001.

5.3   AQAP-110 AND AQAP-150

The military purchase all kinds of equipment. Therefore, NATO publishes standards intended for use by the customer side in large acquisitions, two of them being AQAP-110 and AQAP-150. "AQAP" is an acronym for "Allied Quality Assurance Publication."

AQAP-110 edition 1 was published in March 1993 and is titled "NATO Quality Assurance Requirements for Design, Development and Production." It is basically ISO 9001 with some additions. AQAP-110 has the same structure of its requirements as has ISO 9001, and AQAP-110 basically just says "ISO requirements apply." AQAP-110 replaces the older AQAP-1 standard and, like it, contains no software-specific requirements.

AQAP-150 was also published in March 1993. Its title is "NATO Quality Assurance Requirements for Software Development." AQAP-150 replaces the older AQAP-13. It is intended for use either together with AQAP-110 or on its own in acquisitions that include software development.

Since AQAP-150 is software-specific, we should perhaps compare it to ISO 9000-3. The first difference is that AQAP-150 is a *standard*, while ISO 9000-3 is a *guideline*. ISO 9000-3 says "should," while AQAP-150 says "shall." AQAP-150 is strongly focused on project-specific issues, and in essence it contains requirements on the contents of a "Software Quality Assurance Plan" and on the activities controlled by the plan. AQAP-150 is vague on such things as quality policy, management review, contract review, internal quality audits, and training. Also, it says very little about maintenance. Apart from this, AQAP-150 differs from ISO 9000-3 only in details.

5.4 MIL-STD-498

The U.S. Department of Defense is one of the world's major purchasers of software development. Thus, the DoD is able to enforce a certain uniformity among its suppliers regarding the management and development of software. In December 1994 MIL-STD-498 became the major instrument for this, merging the earlier standards DOD-STD-2167A and DOD-STD-7935 into one. DOD-STD-2167A was aimed at embedded systems, while DOD-STD-7935 was aimed at information system software.

MIL-STD-498, titled "Military Standard Software Development and Documentation," is a detailed prescription of the software development process a supplier is required to run. The standard describes what activities to perform, what documents to produce, and what checks to make. The requirements are on a very detailed level; for example, the exact contents of a "Software Design Description" and 21 other documents are specified.

MIL-STD-498 covers ISO 9001 paragraph 4.4, "Design control," in more than 100 pages of detailed requirements. The standard also covers parts of ISO 9001 paragraphs 4.5, "Document and data control," 4.6, "Purchasing," 4.14, "Corrective and preventive action," 4.15, "Handling, storage, packaging, preservation and delivery," and 4.17, "Internal quality audits."

I have had the opportunity to see the predecessor, DOD-STD-2167A, used in several large software acquisitions, and I found that it described a development model quite useful for large projects. This kind of standard can cause problems when it is imposed on a supplier who has not used it previously. If the supplier already has a suitable development model in operation, it should be used, since it is to no one's advantage to force a change to the MIL-STD-498 model for one contract only. The standard is difficult to grasp, and there may be misunderstandings when attempting to use it for the first time.

The requirements in MIL-STD-498 are intended to be tailored by the customer before imposing them on a supplier. This is especially important for small and medium-sized projects, where the standard can easily become oppressive. For DOD-STD-2167A, however, it seemed that the customers tended to require that the suppliers describe their development models in terms of tailoring the standard.

References

[Bamford 1993] R. C. Bamford and W. J. Deibler, "Comparing, contrasting ISO 9001 and the SEI capability maturity model," *IEEE Computer*, October 1993.

[Paulk 1994] M. C. Paulk, R. C. Bamford, and W. J. Deibler, "Basis of contrast between ISO 9001 and SEI capability maturity model challenged," *IEEE Computer*, February 1994.

[Paulk 1993] M. C. Paulk, "Comparing ISO 9001 and the capability maturity model for software," *Software Quality Journal,* vol. 2, pp. 245–256, 1993.

[Paulk 1995] M. C. Paulk, "How ISO 9001 compares with the CMM," *IEEE Software,* January 1995.

[Coallier 1994] F. Coallier, "How ISO 9001 fits into the software world," *IEEE Software,* January 1994.

BUILDING A QUALITY SYSTEM FOR SOFTWARE

6.1 WHAT IS A QUALITY SYSTEM?

Quality system: The organizational structure, responsibilities, procedures, processes and resources for implementing quality management.

Quality management: That aspect of the overall management function that determines and implements the quality policy.

Quality: The totality of features and characteristics of a product or service that bear on its ability to satisfy stated and implied needs.

The definitions above were taken from ISO 8402-1986 "Quality—Vocabulary." The definitions seem to say that the quality system implements the implementation of the quality policy. Did anyone follow that?

Let's try it in English instead. A *quality system* is the organizational structure and so on, which controls and influences the quality of a supplier's products and services. *Quality* is what makes your customer happy.

Virtually everything in a software development organization influences quality, so in practice the quality system in a software development organization is *the means for managing the software development*. Some examples of what may be parts of a quality system for software:

- Schedule and agenda for executive meetings
- Assignments of authorities and responsibilities in the company
- Procedures for project management
- Templates for documents
- Procedures for reviews and tests
- Procedures for handling customer complaints
- Records of employee training
- Procedures for internal audits
- Procedures for handling changes to specifications and programs
- The central product library for software

What, then, is a sufficient quality system to fulfill ISO 9001? This is a question I frequently used to hear. Managers would ask me: "If we do like this, would that satisfy ISO 9001?" "Well," I would answer, "it depends. It is difficult to say... I would have to know more about your company." I felt very uncomfortable with this kind of answer. I ought to be able to say yes or no, oughtn't I? But after a while, I realized that the answer was exactly right: "It depends." What is right for one organization is not necessarily right for the another.

The basic requirement of a quality system is that it works. If an external auditor can see that your quality system works, he or she would probably only be able to find minor things to criticize.

6.2 DO WE NEED A QUALITY SYSTEM FOR SOFTWARE?

Some of the most successful software ever marketed was created without the tiniest pretense of a quality system. This is how you do it: Take three bright programmers fresh out of college. Put them in a garage in California and wait. The kids then have all kinds of fantastic ideas and program them, mostly in assembler language "on the bare metal." Then you sell the programs and get *very* rich.

So why bother with a quality system? Well, there are a few possible reasons:

- Your customers may require that your software works.

- You may want to modify the software.

- You may have to convince your customer beforehand that you will be able to deliver a suitable product.

- You may have to hire programmers who have families and private lives, and who are not prepared to work day and night for three years.

- The original whiz kids may quit and start a business of their own.

- You may even have product liabilities.

If you want to know what you'll get and when you'll get it, you had better have a quality system of some sort. Otherwise, why not try the garage in California?

An intelligent application of the requirements in ISO 9001 will make a software supplier better, the operative word here being "intelligent." For an informally managed organization to lift itself to the ISO 9001 standard must be done carefully. There is much that can go wrong.

6.3   BUILDING THE QUALITY SYSTEM

So let's assume that you are in a business where it matters whether software products are reliable, arrive on time, and can be modified. Let's further assume that in some way management has come to the conclusion that it is important for the company to be up to the ISO 9001 standard. You have been assigned the task of making this happen, so you have to find out how to do it.

6.3.1 WHO SHOULD DO IT?

Don't start a project team or task force of low-level staff off with orders to create and establish a quality system. They will eventually fail, since what they create is wrong and will not be accepted by the organization.

To create, establish, and maintain a quality system is a task for line management. In my view, issuing directives, assigning authority and responsibility, and so on is the most important part of a line manager's job. This is not always understood by the managers; I sometimes see managers who happily spend their time making promises to customers, hiring people, twisting the arms of project leaders, and jumping into firefighting top-priority task forces. Instead, they ought to create a way for their subordinates to work that would make the firefighting and arm-twisting unnecessary.

So it's the line managers who shall build the quality system. Of course, they may use subordinates to help, but each manager should take responsibility for the specific part of the quality system that is unique for his or her area. Managers should also cooperate around that part of the quality system which is above them.

This is also a test of the most important success factor for quality system building: *management commitment*. If the managers on different levels do not feel that the quality system is important and *right*, it will never be built.

The most successful approach I have seen was this: An active and very persuasive quality manager planned the work and coached the line managers. The quality manager prepared and supported the line managers' work by preparing example documents and suggesting actions. He bullied the managers to spend nights and weekends working out how they actually wanted to run the company. When they knew, they could bring in other staff to help with the details.

When the quality manager felt that the company's quality system was in operation, he brought in two external consultants to conduct an internal quality audit to ISO 9001. The consultants found a few things to correct and amend. After this was done, the company was certified to ISO 9001 without any nonconformance noted.

6.3.2 STEP 1: RESPONSIBILITY, AUTHORITY, AND INTERFACES

When management is committed to building a quality system, I suggest that the next step is to iron out the responsibilities, authorities, and interfaces. Your organization is probably defined somewhat informally. Usually, one finds some responsibilities defined, authorities more rarely. There are a few questions to answer:

- Who keeps an eye on X and takes action when needed?

- Who decides about Y?

- What is the formal relation between organization X and organization Y? Which side is in charge of what? Which items are delivered between the organizations?

When all such questions are answered, you will actually *know your company*. Then you can continue looking at more detailed procedures for the actual day-to-day operations.

When management at last knows all about the responsibilities, authorities, and interfaces, this knowledge is documented and disseminated to those concerned. A person who has a responsibility and/or authority must know it, and must be able to find where it is documented.

6.3.3 STEP 2: DIFFERENT PROCESSES

In step 2, each different part of the company works out its procedures *under the supervision of its management.*

Normally, few procedures must be invented. Your company was working before you heard about ISO 9001, so there must exist procedures, although not all are documented. Document existing procedures, and perhaps polish them a little. Establish new procedures where there is a need. Resist the temptation to throw the old procedures away and invent everything anew. If you do that, you may disrupt the operation of the company, and this would delay the quality system considerably. If it worked before, it is probably okay with ISO 9001. If you are sure it should be changed, try to do this modification as a separate activity after the introduction of the quality system. The most likely area in which you will have to add procedures and rules is with regard to records. Software developers rarely recognize the need to keep records; they remember everything important anyhow, and they do not recognize the customer's legitimate need to see records.

6.3.3.1 Executive Management

Document the means for executive management to receive feedback from the operations of the company. For example, a management review of the quality system shall be held regularly. This can be done by having the quality manager present the results from and actions on internal audits and problem analyses in an annual review. The fulfillment of quality goals should also be reviewed.

6.3.3.2 Development

Document how projects are managed, supervised, and planned. Prepare a template for project plans. Document the project manager's authority to prescribe project-specific procedures.

Document a basic development model with activities, document types, reviews, and tests. Prepare templates for documents and procedures for reviews and tests. Include in the procedures rules for what records shall be prepared and kept.

Document procedures for identification, archiving, and change control for documents and programs. Document procedures for error reporting during development.

Document procedures for delivery and installation. Document procedures for archiving, error correction and enhancements after delivery.

A tempting shortcut would be to decide that each new project shall define its own procedures and standards, and document them in the development and quality plans. Then we don't need to do very much, do we? The problem of ISO 9001 compliance suddenly falls into the laps of the project managers.

First of all, it would be inefficient to have each project manager reinvent old wheels. Second, the project managers would, in practice, use procedures and standards from old projects, so there would be an *informal* common quality system. Third, if you are to get a certificate of compliance to ISO 9001, that certificate will be about your company, not any individual project.

For an auditor, it is a matter of judgment how much you might be allowed to leave to individual projects. Note, however, that if two projects are using the same practices, procedures, or rules, then the practices, procedures, and rules constitute something common which shall be documented outside the projects.

6.3.3.3 Quality Assurance

Document plans and procedures for internal quality audits.

Document procedures for the collection of statistics, problem reports, and other records, and the subsequent analyses to find weaknesses in work processes. Document how actions are initiated and recorded.

6.3.3.4 Sales

The sales department should document the sales process, and especially the contract review. Perhaps there are customer satisfaction investigations or reception of customer complaints. Document procedures.

You might notice that ISO 9001 is not about sales. The title does not mention sales, nor is there any mention of it in the text of the standard. Still, an auditor will, by inference, require that activities supporting design, development, production, installation, and servicing be under proper control.

6.3.3.5 Personnel

Usually, the personnel department keeps employee files. This may be a good place to keep training records also. Personnel may also be in charge of enforcing regular discussions between managers and subordinates about training needs, and the subsequent updating of training records. Document procedures for this.

Also, procedures for the recruitment and introduction of new employees should be documented.

6.3.4 SWITCHING OVER

Usually, it is best if a quality system can be introduced step by step over a period of time.

If the new quality system is introduced through an

abrupt "switchover," or if your projects stretch over a long period of time, there is the question of what to do with ongoing projects. Presumably, the old projects do not follow quality systems that are up to ISO 9001. It is important to notice that your company cannot claim to have a quality system in accordance with ISO 9001 if there are projects running that do not fulfill the requirements of the standard.

On the other hand, the old projects do not have to follow the new quality system. A good way to handle this situation is to modify the plans for the old projects so that *the rest* of the projects are conducted in a manner which satisfies the standard. There is, of course, no need to redo the parts of the projects that are already finished.

6.4 BUT WHAT WILL THE PROGRAMMERS SAY?

Myth: "Programmers are creative individuals who can't be managed."

I sometimes hear managers voice concern regarding their programmers' aversion to every kind of management, rule, and paperwork. "We have tried. We had a consultant prepare a comprehensive program development handbook in three volumes, but we were unable to make the programmers use it."

I have frequently worked for the customer side with contracts that include software development. Each time I have been obliged to criticize the supplier for lack of management and procedures for software development, a programmer has taken me aside to tell me "It was really good that you said that. We have been pestering management for several years now, saying that we must establish rules and standards for our software development."

I have often been involved with the introduction of formalized development processes for software, with rules and paperwork. I have *never* heard a programmer say "What a bloody nuisance this is! Paper and rules will curtail our creativity and prevent us from doing our job" or anything else in that vein.

The programmers will be no problem at all. Rather, they will help enthusiastically with the preparation of specification templates, programming rules, and reviewing procedures; under two conditions, though:

1. The templates, rules, procedures, and so forth are introduced with the aim of supporting the programmers and helping them to do a still better job.

2. The templates, rules, procedures, and so forth are the *right ones*.

For a professional to be forced to follow a rule that does not have any reasonable purpose is both insulting and demoralizing. Even worse is the not uncommon case when the rule incurs extra cost at the same time as it forces the programmer to do a bad job.

It is important that the right people prepare instructions for software development. Often, a software organization has one or two "gurus" to whom everyone will go when they have problems with specifications or programs. Let those "gurus" prepare the rules and procedures. Do not leave this work to people who are not software experts themselves, and do not use outside consultants who want to do the whole job.

6.5 THE CERTIFICATION PROCESS

6.5.1 PREPARING FOR CERTIFICATION

So now your company has a quality system that is up to ISO 9001 (you believe). Why not get a third-party certificate to that effect? Actually, it might be a good idea to decide about the certification when starting the work with the quality system. In that way, everyone would see a specific goal for the work, and it is also easier to get things going if you can refer to a "foreign power," the certification body, that will eventually come to inspect the result.

The following describes how certification of a software developing company might happen. Remember that I am using international terminology. In the U.S., "registration" is used for "certification," and certification bodies are called "registrars."

Some companies are in a great hurry to get a certificate immediately after they have built the quality system, often because the manager has set a goal of certification by a certain date. They get disappointed. After you have put a quality system in operation, you have to wait some time before attempting certification. This is because certification bodies do not certify "good intentions." You must show that your procedures are in operation by, for example, having a couple of projects apply them from start to finish.

How long will it take to build and implement a quality system for software development? This, of course, depends on your situation when you start and on the length of your projects. If you only run long projects, you might take on a short project only to be able to show the certifiers your ability to apply the complete quality system. In general, you might be wise to allow one or two years' time for building the quality system and collecting evidence of your ability to apply all parts of it.

The first step is to choose a certification body. A list of certification bodies (registrars) accredited by the U.S. accreditation authority, RAB, is available from:

Registrar Accreditation Board
611 East Wisconsin Avenue
P.O. Box 3005
Milwaukee, WI 53201-3005
Phone: 414-272 8575
Fax: 414-765 8661

This list does not indicate which of the certification bodies are prepared to take on the certification of software development. In other countries, go to the national accreditation authorities for similar lists.

The certification body does not have to be accredited by RAB. For example, TickIT certifications are not accredited by RAB, so if you want a TickIT certificate, you will have to go for a certificate under accreditation by the British accreditation authority, NACCB. A list of accredited TickIT certification bodies is available from:

NACCB
Audley House
13 Palace Street
London SW1E 5HS
England
Phone: +44 171-233 7111
Fax: +44 171-233 5115

Elicit bids from a couple of certification companies. As the basis for the bid, they will require some information about your company, for example:

• Size

• Number of sites

• Scope of your business

Choose a certification body from the following criteria, among others:

• Price

• References from other software-developing customers of the certification body

• The documented software competence of the certification body's auditors

Insist that your software development be certified only by auditors who themselves have thorough experience in developing software. Registered TickIT auditors are preferable.

Many European certification bodies offer as a service a "precertification": a brief audit to ascertain whether your company has any major deficiencies with regards to ISO 9001. Don't use this service if you don't have to. Certification bodies are not allowed to give advice, so the result of such a brief "precertification" will not be very helpful. The auditors might say, for example, "Your document control is insufficient, and there are weaknesses in your design control." They are not allowed to suggest what you should do about it. It is much better to find someone competent in ISO 9001 and software to do a thorough audit of your operation, and to produce a comprehensive report with detailed advice as to what you should do. The reason why certification bodies are not allowed to give advice is that the auditors could not be neutral about a quality system prepared in accordance with their advice.

When you have contracted a suitable certification body and agreed about the time for the certification audit, inform your staff clearly about the certification itself and about what is required from them. Most of us are not used to having strangers coming to us and asking intricate questions about our way of work. It is easy to become intimidated in such situations if one is not prepared for the experience, and it is unnecessary. One of the advantages of having someone from the outside make an audit as preparation for certification is that this tends to make people more used to the idea, so at the certification audit they are able to show their best side. Tell people not to lie or hide anything, but tell them to be careful about what they tell the auditors. If one lets oneself go, the connection between brain and mouth may overload, resulting in an unnecessarily bad impression.

If people appear really terrified at the prospect of a certification audit, it may be a good idea to educate them.

Describe what an audit is about, how it is done, and how to behave as an auditee. Perhaps run an audit interview in front of an audience so that people get a feel for it.

You should also tell your staff about the contents and implications of ISO 9001, but don't send them all to courses about ISO 9001. The only ones who have to know ISO 9001 are the managers and others involved in the design of the quality system. They create a quality system that fulfills the standard, and the staff only have to see that quality system, not the standard itself.

Don't choose a time for the certification:

- When you just have had a reorganization

- When half the programmers are away on a course

- When you are in a critical phase in a project

6.5.2 THE CERTIFICATION AUDIT

When the time and duration of the certification audit have been agreed upon, the certification body will prepare an *audit program*, detailing what department and what type of staff they want to meet and when. The following functions will surely be in the program:

- The managing director

- The quality manager

- All department heads

- Personnel, training staff

- Project managers and software engineers on ongoing projects

The first day of the certification audit, there will be some trepidation on the part of your staff. It is "graduation" after a long period of preparation. On the positive side, there will be curiosity and eagerness to show one's work and ability. On the negative side, there will be nervousness and a feeling that the certification body is trespassing.

The first day starts with an *entry meeting*, where the certification auditors meet with company management and with the persons who will act as guides during the day. At the entry meeting, the lead auditor will explain the purpose of the audit and present the auditors. Your representatives will introduce themselves. The audit program will be discussed and possibly changed. An office will be made available to the auditors for internal meetings. An overview of the company will be presented, possibly followed by a brief tour of the premises.

Then the audit proper starts. The goal of the audit is to ascertain that your quality system is up to ISO 9001, and that it is implemented in the day-to-day operations of your company. The auditors will split up, each with a guide, and go out to interview different people. The interviews will normally take place at the interviewee's place of work. The auditor will be interested in how that person works, and what documents are available. A good auditor will not start asking questions from the standard or from a checklist. Rather, the auditor wants the interviewee to tell in his or her own words what he or she is doing. After that, the auditor will ask a few questions. With a manager, he or she will ask, for example:

- "How do you manage your department?"

- "How do you get feedback from your staff?"

- "What records are there from your control?"

When the interviewee mentions a document, the auditor will say "Show me!" This is a conditioned reflex of all quality auditors. To listen to people telling you about their work is interesting, but it gains substance only when you can inspect something tangible (e.g., a specification, a program, or a review record,.

At the end of the day, the auditors will meet to compare

notes, and afterwards there will be a meeting between the auditors and the company managers, where the auditors will present any nonconformances discovered during the day. You will then have the opportunity to correct the nonconformances and have the auditors clear them during the audit. You will be required to at least produce an action plan for the nonconformances.

Some nonconformances cannot be corrected immediately; for example, if some major activities have not been conducted such as internal audits or design reviews. Also, even if you are able to correct all nonconformances concerning, say, document control, the auditors may still raise a general nonconformance regarding this quality element. The auditors only do sampling. If they find many nonconformances in a certain area through sampling, they will assume that there are many undetected nonconformances for every one they uncover. It is then not enough to fix the problems the auditors happened to find. You will have to go through the sampled area thoroughly to ensure that there are no nonconformances left which could be found in another sampling.

Each morning there will be an "entry meeting," when you will have the opportunity to present corrections and/or action plans for nonconformances.

Then comes the last day of the audit, and in the afternoon there is an *exit meeting* planned. At this meeting, the auditors will tell you the outcome of the audit. There are three possibilities:

1. The auditors will recommend immediate certification. In this case, there must be no unresolved nonconformances. This is a rare case, but I have seen it happen.

2. The auditors will recommend certification pending the satisfactory resolution of all remaining nonconformances within a certain time limit (e.g., three months). The certification body must be able to confirm the fact that the nonconformances have been corrected, either from docu-

ments received from the company or through a visit by an auditor.

3. The auditors cannot recommend certification. You will have to work on your quality system and its implementation in the organization and then apply for certification anew.

Hopefully, your case will be 1 or 2 above, so you will after some time receive an impressive certificate saying that your company is now a member of the enviable group of software suppliers who fulfill the requirements of the international quality standard ISO 9001.

6.5.3 MAINTAINING A CERTIFICATE

The certificate you just received and put up on the boardroom wall is valid for a certain period of time, usually three years. After that time, you will have to apply for certification and do it all over again. Hopefully, the process will be much simpler this time.

So when you have received your certificate, you can lean back and relax for three years. How wonderful, after all the overtime you put in to get the quality system going!

Forget it; the auditors will be back soon. In your contract with the certification body, it is stated that they will do regular audits twice a year during the time of the certificate. Often, an organization is kept on its toes until the certification is done, but then the reaction comes, and the disciplined way of working is replaced with the usual sloppiness. That's why the certification body will be back to check that your company is not one of these organizations. These regular surveillance audits are less comprehensive than the certification audit, and usually the auditors concentrate on different areas of your quality system each time.

During the term of the certificate, you can still lose it. In some situations, the certification body has the obligation or authority to withdraw your certificate. Examples are:

- If you fail to correct within the prescribed time a non-conformance found in a surveillance audit

- If you use the certificate improperly in your marketing, for example, indicating that this is a certificate of the quality of your products

- If you don't pay the bills from the certification body

A major reorganization or a merger with another company can make the certificate invalid, but often this can be avoided if the certification body is kept involved in the change so that its auditors can audit the new organization and confirm the certificate.

6.6 MAINTAINING A QUALITY SYSTEM

A quality system that is not maintained will quickly degenerate. Responsibilities and authorities will change as people move around in the organization, rules will become obsolete because better methods have been found, and so on. Of course, the certification body returns twice a year to check up on you, but they only do sampling, and you are not allowed to use their audits as a means for finding out what has to be done; you must find out for yourself.

You have four main tools for maintaining the quality system:

1. Internal quality audits. Aside from being "police actions," making sure that people adhere to the quality system, your internal quality audits should be aimed at finding out if something is wrong with the system itself and looking for opportunities to improve it. For example, the fact that someone is not following a procedure may be an indication that the procedure should be changed.

2. Your continuing improvement activities. ISO 9001 paragraph 4.14 requires that you actively collect and analyze information about problems and shortcomings in order to find possible improvements. The standard further requires that you have some means for implementing and following up decisions from this activity.

3. Suggestions and complaints from your staff using the quality system. Make clear to everyone that suggestions and complaints are *welcome*; make it easy to document suggestions and complaints (on the system or using a form), and make sure that people know *where* to go with them. The suggestions and complaints can be the input into the process of 2.

4. Post mortem analysis. It is a good idea to sit down immediately after the finish of a project and discuss what was good and what wasn't about the way the project was run, with rules and procedures and so forth. Write a short report and enter it into 2.

Remember: If you don't improve, you deteriorate. To stay on top, you must improve all the time.

Applying ISO 9000 to Software Projects

Introduction

ISO 9000, as we have already seen, evolved in a world far from software. More recently, special pains have been taken to make it appropriate for software. Still, there are some things missing twixt the ISO 9000 cup and our lip.

In this book, we collect those things in this section. Applying ISO 9000 to software, which seems so simple in the 9000-3 and TickIT documents, is not. It is here that we present the notion of applying ISO 9000 to software projects, a process that we would assert requires considerable tailoring and interpretation. (We are not alone in that assertion; Avison [1994] says things like "...ISO 9001 is a useful starting point for quality improvement ... but ... its usefulness and effectiveness is limited"; and "The standard is based on conformance rather than effectiveness of an organization ... Indeed, there are those who are simply paying lip service to the procedures created to satisfy the standard.")

There are two major succeeding chapters in this portion of the book. In Chapter 7, we break down software into several types of projects. Each of those project types, we say there, must be treated differently. ISO 9000-3 cannot be applied uncritically across all these project types—it must, as we have said above, be interpreted for each of these contexts.

The types of projects we present here are differentiated by project size, project application domain, project criticality, and project innovativeness. Each of those project types (which we will further define in what follows) demands different interpretations of ISO 9000.

It is in Chapter 8 that we provide those interpretations. Using the organizational framework presented in ISO 9000-3, one which is heavily dependent on the software life cycle, we present a menu of techniques for building quality software and a matrix of choices for when to use each technique on each type of project (employing the types defined in Chapter 7).

The result may appear more confusing than the simple

direction provided by ISO 9000-3. But to those who truly understand what software is all about, that should not be surprising. If software is indeed "the most complex activity ever engaged in by human beings," as many software engineering experts have said, then we should not expect to find simple approaches to employing it as a problem-solving device.

Besides, even for the most rudimentary of occupations, there is normally a complex array of tools available. And each of those tools is to be used on a particular type of project. Would the woodworker try to use a ball peen hammer and a Phillips screwdriver for all the activities of woodworking? Why should we expect the software professional to use a simple collection of tools independent of the nature of the project on which they are to be used?

The material that follows is not, however, without controversy. The project types, and the menus of techniques vs. types, are not part of the traditional software engineering literature. You will not be able to confirm or deny the taxonomy of types, or the menu of choices, by going elsewhere to get a second opinion. In all fairness, we do not expect the reader to accept our taxonomy and our menu without second thoughts and reservations. What we do hope is that the reader who has problems with our choices will think further, and develop comfortable choices of his or her own. It is vital, we believe, to differentiate projects by their type. It is vital, we also believe, to apply solution approaches judicially, considering the nature of the project type. What we would like to sell you here is the notion of options and choice. Whether you buy into our specific taxonomy, and our specific menus, is far less important. If you do not, we encourage you to develop your own.

With that as introduction, let us move on.

Reference

[Avison 1994] D. E. Avison, H. U. Shah, and D. N. Wilson, "Software Quality Standards in Practice: The Limitations of Using ISO-9001 to Support Software Development," *Software Quality Journal*, vol. 3, pp. 105–111, 1994.

PROJECT DIFFERENCES AND QUALITY: DIFFERENT STROKES FOR DIFFERENT FOLKS

$\mathbf{F}$or decades now, software research has studied ways of approaching the problems of software with a "one size fits all" mentality. Each new concept to emerge from the halls of research has been hailed as the solution to the difficulties of all software.

There are two major problems with this approach. The first is that there has been far too much "hailing" and far too little measuring. If a bright research mind conceives of an idea, and further analysis makes it look promising, all too often the next research step taken is to write a paper hailing the idea and advocating its adoption in practice. The problem here is premature hailing. Analytic reasoning is simply not sufficient testing to support advocacy. It takes empirical measurement, evaluation of the new idea in a somewhat realistic setting, to determine whether praise is really appropriate. And there has been far too little empirical, evaluative research in the software field [JSS 1995].

The second major problem with this approach is the notion that new ideas will be applicable to all software. There is emerging evidence that different ideas are necessary for different types of projects. Early in the history of the field, when the pace of progress was extremely rapid and almost any new idea was a good one, it may have made sense to assume that new ideas had value software-wide, but that time has long since passed. It is essential that new ideas not only be evaluated empirically, but that they be evaluated in a setting which allows decisions to be made about just when they might be applicable.

The remainder of this chapter is an expansion on these ideas. The ideas are essential to the message of this book and our interpretation of ISO 9000. Although there is very little in the standard that speaks of different techniques for different projects, failing to take that approach will be the software equivalent of trying to swat flies with crowbars.

7.1 DOES ONE SIZE FIT ALL?

The question has, of course, already been answered in the preceding section. It is worth repeating here, and spending a little more time on, because the view that different software projects require different approaches is still uncommon in the software field. New methodologies are introduced with the claim that they should be used enterprise-wide. (Unless the enterprise only does one type of software development, this is quite likely to be bad, counterproductive advice.) New maturity models, such as the Software Engineering Institute's, are defined in such a way that they are to be used to measure all software organizations, regardless of the nature of the work they do. (One of the main reasons for opposition to the SEI model is the fact that its processes are required to be employed on small projects as well as large ones.) New standards are advocated without regard to an interpretation of how and when they should be used. (ISO 9000 provides very little tailoring advice for applying its concepts.)

Fortunately, there is a growing understanding of the role of project types in the use of software techniques. Unfortunately, so far that understanding is largely present only among practitioners. One particularly articulate practitioner has said, "Anyone who believes that one size fits all belongs in a pantyhose commercial" [Plauger 1994]. Another, noted as a successful software futurist, says that the shift away from a belief that "all software is essentially the same" is "the most interesting paradigm shift now taking place" [Yourdon 1995]. Most researchers and methodologists have too little understanding of the breadth of software projects to have gained the needed insight. Researchers tend to see the software world through the knothole of small systems programs applications; methodologists tend to see the software world through the knothole of large business applications. It will take a major leap of understanding before all the players in the software field are reading from the same page of music. It is ironic that one researcher, more aware than most of the need for project differentiation, published an article in a leading journal on "Eclectic Design Approaches" tailored to the needs of the projects [Sanden 1989]. The journal, steeped in the traditional one-size-fits-all view, and apparently not having the faintest idea what the author was trying to say, printed the article with the title as "Electric Design Approaches"!

However, the notion of project-specific approaches, particularly from the point of view of differing application domains, is finally beginning to find its way into the more academic literature. Such papers as [Vessey 1995] and [Glass 1992] discuss the problems of forming a taxonomy of applications, and [Vessey 1994] presents the advantages for doing so.

7.2 THE ROLE OF PROJECT SIZE

Probably the most important factor in differentiating between projects is their size. In this book, we divide projects into "large" and "small." That is, of course, an arbitrary and all too black and white distinction. Furthermore, it is very difficult to define what "large" and "small" really mean.

The most popular approach in the software field to discussing project size is the measure "lines of code" (LOC). The total number of lines is counted, procedures and data and comments and all, and then some judgment is made about what that means. LOC approaches are used for estimating project cost and schedule, as well as for measuring project size once the product has been built.

Just as there are many advocates of LOC approaches, there are also many opponents. Probably the most outspoken is Capers Jones, who declares that LOC is a dangerous way to measure anything. He has good reason for his opposition. The same application, coded in a high-level or low-level language, will have vastly different LOC characteristics. There are counting-rule arguments about what really constitutes a "line," and the differences in counting rules can make profound differences in the measurements. Although LOC is easily obtained, it appears to be an unstable way of measuring.

Many who oppose LOC approaches instead support the idea of the "function point" (FP) approach. Function points are functional entities in the problem for which a software project is being organized. Capers Jones, for example, is a strong advocate of FP instead of LOC approaches. But there is a problem with FP as well. If one examines the definition of what constitutes an FP, it is quickly apparent to those knowledgeable in several application domains that the approach is inappropriate for most applications, having meaning largely for business applications focused mainly on data manipulation. Even Capers Jones has invented a parallel metric he calls "feature points," where the traditional FP approach is augmented by some additional counting rules for more algorithmic types of applications.

But all of these counting approaches to measuring project size miss one important fact. What really makes large projects very different from small ones is not so much the nature of the solution (LOC) or the problem (FP), but rather the different project team characteristics of large and small projects. Large projects require a great deal of communication among project participants, best handled by well-defined lines of communication. And those well-defined approaches demand disciplined following and formal definition.

Consider this: Suppose the superman of software were assigned to the most complicated software project of all time. And suppose that superman churned out thousands of lines of correct code per day to solve the thousands of function points presented by the problem. Suppose the end product was measured in gigalines of code. Would that be a large project? By most definitions, it would. But by the one presented here, it would not. One superprogrammer working alone has far fewer communication problems. (Although there is a need to document things the superprogrammer might otherwise forget, that documentation need only be read by the superprogrammer and can employ any conventions the superprogrammer finds useful, regardless of any enterprise standards.) Discipline and formality can be replaced by innovativeness and utility, so long as the appropriate rigor is employed, and so long as the result advances the development of the product.

So, according to this book, project size should be measured in project participants because of the communication lines needed to support a large number of participants. But where do we draw the line between large and small? Here, as we said before, things get arbitrary. In a previous pair of books [Glass 1979, 1992] I took the position that small projects involved five or fewer developers, medium projects involved 6–29, and large ones employed 30 or more. In spite of the fact that there is some data showing that project sizes increased by a factor of 50 from 1980 to 1990, I see no need to change those distinctions here. The largest project I have heard of, employing close to 1000 developers, was done in the 1970s. Perhaps in some of the large, GUI-based, integrated software packages produced by today's micro software houses, those numbers have been eclipsed. But I have not seen the data to support such a belief, and I tend to doubt it. Microsoft only employs 1600 software developers in total (across all projects) [AP 1995]. The evidence I have suggests that large projects in the micro world are trying to stick to the informal approaches of smaller projects and hold team sizes down to make that possible. Lots of overtime appears to be substituting for lots of developers in today's software paradigm in some circles.

Now, having defined small, medium, and large software projects in a book that chooses to differentiate only between small and large ones, we obviously have built ourselves a mapping problem. Here is our resolution to the problem:

Small projects are those involving five or fewer developers. Large projects are those involving 30 or more developers. Projects involving from 6 to 29 people fall into a gray area where judgment must be employed by project leaders to determine what size they consider their project to be. This is not as shocking a "punt" as it may seem. The major distinction in what follows between small and large projects is in the formality of the approaches applied. For example, whereas large projects will use formal organizational approaches for configuration management and quality assurance, small projects will solve those same problems with a much more informal approach. Those 6–29 developer projects, then, should align themselves in the middle of the formality spectrum.

7.3 THE ROLE OF THE APPLICATION DOMAIN

Probably the least understood criterion for differentiating among projects is by their application domain. The reason it is not well understood is that there are few people in the software field who have truly experienced significant projects in more than one or two such domains. Most researchers, as we have mentioned before, have participated in major projects in at most one, and often no, domain.

Because of this lack of expertise in the area of domains, we lack even the most rudimentary tools to distinguish projects by domain. For example, there is no well-accepted taxonomy of application domains at a reasonable level of depth. Research into the topic shows a deplorable confusion in attempts to define such taxonomies—most not only disagree with each other, but further confuse the topic they are trying to clarify [Glass 1993]. There are historic reasons why all of this is so [Glass 1992a], but it does not help—there has been little progress in characterizing the applicability of software techniques to software application domains, largely because the notion of domain remains under-defined. (One interesting exception is the proposal in [Jones 1994], which distinguishes between MIS, systems, commercial [e.g., packages], military, contract/outsourced, and end-user domains).

At the same time, many are convinced that the domain must play a major role in the discussion of software technique applicability. For example, Potts [1993] takes the position that "Requirements definition will probably not improve unless we begin to use domain-specific notations and analysis heuristics"; McSharry [1994] says that "a domain-specific, product-based improvement program is the place to start for measurable results"; and the USNRC [1990] points out the need for "different types of abstraction and different language requirements arising from differences in the representation of application information."

Nevertheless, progress in achieving domain-specific approaches is terribly slow. Potts [1993] notes that "most software engineering research keeps focusing on general mechanisms and languages." Do researchers really believe that the same methodology can deal with database-focused business applications and device-focused real-time ones, for example? Can we employ object-oriented approaches just as readily on compiler development as on GUI software? Does today's crop of CASE tools help the scientific developer as much as they help the business application developer? Although the answers to these questions are muddy in the mid to late 1990s, the answer is quite likely to be "no" more often than "yes."

What to do, then, in this book? We believe it is vital to differentiate among the technologies we present here by application domain as well as size and other project characteristics, but the tools—the taxonomies—for doing so are lacking.

Fortunately, there is a traditional fallback position. Almost from the beginnings of the software field, we have used a rudimentary taxonomy to distinguish among applications. It is not very satisfying in its precision, but at least it is still generally accepted and understood. That taxonomy distinguishes among:

- Business applications, focusing on the needs of the business back room, such as accounting and information systems

- Scientific applications, focusing on the needs of enterprise scientists, often characterized by mathematical algorithms

- Systems applications, focusing on the needs of software developers and consisting of the tools software people need

- Real-time applications, focusing on the needs of problems whose solutions interact with a rapidly ongoing world, often characterized by servicing interactions among hardware devices

(We do not use the previously mentioned taxonomy from [Jones 1994] because it is not yet generally accepted, and it mixes application domains (e.g., MIS, systems) and project modes (e.g., outsourced, end-user)).

In the spirit of ISO 9000, this is probably yet another example of a necessary but far from sufficient taxonomy! However, in the absence of anything better, that is the one we employ in this book.

7.4 THE ROLE OF PROJECT CRITICALITY

If size is the most important factor in distinguishing between projects, and application domain is the least well understood, how can we characterize project criticality? Here is where we find the most vital need for differentiation.

Critical software is software whose functioning effects human lives and/or huge amounts of money. Critical software is software whose failure would be characterized as a disaster. Given this definition, critical software is uncommon in the total world of software, but it is the kind of software for which attention to success is unavoidable.

What are some examples of critical software? Flight control software on the aircraft you are aboard. Banking software that handles international interbank transfers. Medical software that displays patient care data. Monitoring software that checks the functioning of nuclear power plants. Even the software that controls the computer that controls the antilock braking system in your personal automobile. As you can see, critical software comes in all sizes, all domains, and all walks of life!

Where is the focus of concern for critical software? It is largely one particular aspect of quality, reliability. Critical software simply cannot be unreliable. In the division of technologies by project characteristics, virtually all of those techniques that can enhance reliability should be employed—to the nth degree—on critical projects.

There is nothing new about the notion of critical software. Flight software has been on aircraft since the 1960s and perhaps before. Control software has been employed in rail systems for a similar period of time, both on the trains and at remote control sites. Fortunately, over the years we have learned a considerable amount about how to make critical software reliable. That will be the focus of attention in those portions of this book devoted to critical applications.

7.5   THE ROLE OF PROJECT INNOVATION

This project characteristic is a new one, even to me. I don't mean that I haven't recognized that some projects are more innovative than others (for example, I participated in space software projects in the 1950s and 1960s). What I mean is that it was only recently that I came to realize that these kinds of projects also require approaches that are different from those of other projects. That insight came from some colleagues and correspondents who were helping me in the development of an earlier book, *Software Creativity* [Glass 1995]. (Their contribution is specifically cited and discussed in the closing portions of that book.)

What they pointed out was that when they closed the doors of their offices and worked on some software project which taxed their mental processes because it was unlike anything they had ever done before, they threw away all the lessons they had learned about building good software and employed all the techniques they told others not to use!

The more I thought about that insight, the more I realized my correspondents were onto something. How often have we heard the story of a software developer who, pressured by some kind of external factor, went straight to the heart of software development, neglecting all the disciplined, formal processes that those in the field have advocated for over three decades now?   Is this just foolishness being played out over and over again? Or is there something more serious going on?

I have come to believe that my correspondents and those

pressured software developers are right. There are times when all the wisdom in the field must be questioned if not overturned, and straightforward (perhaps even crude) devices employed to get the job done. In a way, this should not surprise us. The software field is a new one. The accumulated wisdom in the field is only a few decades old. Little of it has really ever been empirically tested. Perhaps, these correspondents are saying, some of that accumulated wisdom is either momentarily discardable, or even wrong.

In what follows in this book, we use (for the first time) this new distinction. Typically, innovative projects are those in which the problem is new and different. (Much less often, innovative projects might involve new and different solution approaches.) If your mind is wrapped around *whether* you can solve the problem at all, the nuances of solution approaches seem far less important. It is in these kinds of projects that the notion of formality, the notion of discipline, falls furthest away from helpfulness. It is here that creativity comes to the fore, and nothing can be allowed to get in its way.

References

[JSS 1995] Issue of the *Journal of System Software* devoted to the notion of a shortage of, and need for, evaluative research, Jan. 1995.

[Glass 1992] Robert L. Glass and Iris Vessey, "Toward a Taxonomy of Application Domains: History," *Journal of Systems and Software*, pp. 189–199, Feb. 1992.

[Plauger 1994] P. J. Plauger, *Programming on Purpose*, Englewood Cliffs, N.J.: Prentice Hall, 1994.

[Sanden 1989] Bo Sanden, "The Case for Electric [sic] Design of Real-Time Software," *IEEE Transactions on Software Engineering*, SE-15 (3), pp. 360–362.

[Vessey 1994] Iris Vessey and Robert L. Glass, "Rethinking the Nature of Application System Development," working paper, Pennsylvania State University; an informal version of this paper was published as "Application-Based Methodologies" in *Information Systems Management*, Fall, 1994.

[Vessey 1995] Iris Vessey and Robert L. Glass, "Contemporary Application Domain Taxonomies," *IEEE Software*, July 1995.

[Yourdon 1995] Ed Yourdon, "'Pastists' and Futurists: Taking Stock at Mid-Decade," *Guerilla Programmer* vol. 2, no. 1, January, 1995.

[AP 1995] "Living in a Microsoft World," special issue of the *American Programmer,* Feb. 1995.

[Glass 1979] Robert L. Glass, *Software Reliability Guidebook*, Englewood Cliffs, N.J.: Prentice Hall, 1979.

[Glass 1992] Robert L. Glass, *Building Quality Software*, Englewood Cliffs, N.J.: Prentice Hall, 1992.

[Glass 1992a] Robert L. Glass and Iris Vessey, "Toward a Taxonomy of Software Application Domains: History," *Journal of Systems and Software*, Feb. 1992.

[Glass 1993] Robert L. Glass and Iris Vessey, "Towards Taxonomies of Application Domains: Work in Progress," *Proceedings of the Second Annual Conference on Achieving Quality in Software*, Venice, Oct. 1993; ([Vessey 1995] is a more complete version of this paper).

[Glass 1995] Robert L. Glass, *Software Creativity,* Englewood Cliffs, N.J.: Prentice Hall, 1995.

[Jones 1994] Capers Jones, *Assessment and Control of Software Risks*, Yourdon Press, 1994.

[McSharry 1994] Maureen McSharry, "Can You Tell Me When You've Improved?" (quoting Frank McGarry, then of NASA-Goddard's Software Engineering Laboratory), *The Software Practitioner*, March 1994.

[Potts 1993] Colin Potts, "Software-Engineering Research Revisited," *IEEE Software*, Sept. 1993.

[USNRC 1990] U.S. National Research Council: Computer Science and Technology Board, "Scaling Up: A Research Agenda for Software Engineering," *Communications of the ACM*, March 1990.

THE QUALITY SYSTEM AND THE LIFE CYCLE

$\mathbf{I}$n the previous chapter, we saw that applying ISO 9000 to a specific project is a nontrivial task. There are many different kinds of projects with many different needs, and the generalities that the standard mentions must be interpreted into a specific approach for a specific project.

In this section of the book, we will attempt to bridge that gap between the generalized standard and specific project needs. In order to do that, we will use the organizational framework of ISO 9000-3, and indicate within that framework what should be done to build quality software on specific kinds of projects.

ISO 9000-3 organizes the quality system material into three sections:

• The quality system framework

• Quality system life-cycle activities

• Quality system supporting activities

In this chapter, we deal with the latter two items. We accept the ISO 9000-3 breakdown of the life cycle into

requirements, design and implementation, testing and validation, acceptance, replication/delivery/installation, and
maintenance. (Note that *Building Quality Software*, the
companion book to this volume for those who want more
depth than is presented here, uses a slightly different life
cycle, but the mapping between the two is obvious and
straightforward. In fact, there are many variations in defining the life cycle—your own view of it may be different still—
but ISO 9000-3 is reasonably flexible on life-cycle definition.
The reader need only map his or her definition onto that of
9000-3 in order to use the standard—and this book).

Although 9000-3 makes a crisp separation between life-
cycle activities and supporting activities, in this section we
include them all together. The reason is that the form of the
discussion is the same for both: we present first what ISO
9000-3 requires for the subject (e.g., requirements or supporting activities), next the issues surrounding that subject
(topics on which there are unresolved questions), then a discussion of techniques for achieving quality for that subject,
and finally a summary in which the needs of 9000-3 are compared with the techniques presented, and the techniques differentiated (as to their desirability) by project type.

It is important to note here that ISO 9000-3 is heavily
focused on planning activities. It specifically mentions (in its
section 5.4.1) a development plan, a quality plan, a configuration management plan, an integration plan, and a test
plan. Other sections of the standard mention additional
plans (e.g., its section 5.10.2 mentions a maintenance plan).
In this chapter, however, we focus not so much on planning
but on doing. The techniques mentioned above are things to
be done when building a quality software product. We do
that because it is necessary to know what is to be done
before it is possible to document the doing in a plan.

In the material that follows, then, there is a menu of
choices for what can be done on a software project to achieve
a quality product. Accompanying that menu is a guide to
using the menu—advice on what project types most need (or

least need) each of the various activities. Using that approach, we believe, makes it possible to construct a project-specific quality approach and plan that maximizes the chances of project success.

8.1 REQUIREMENTS

ISO 9000 is oriented toward purchased software. That is no more evident anywhere than in section 5.3 of ISO 9000-3, where the topic is "Purchaser's requirements specification."

But traditionally, software needs a requirements definition activity whether it is developed for sale in the marketplace or for the use of a specific customer. The requirements for software developed for sale will probably be derived from a market analysis; for software for internal use or by external contract, from interactions with the customer. The difference between the traditional approach and that stated in 9000-3 is in who writes the requirements specification. Although 9000-3 provides for the possibility that the "supplier" (of the software) will write the specification "in close cooperation with the purchaser," the fundamental assumption is that it is the "purchaser's requirements specification."

In any case, 9000-3 requires that this requirements specification have this content:

- Functional requirements (these should be "complete and unambiguous")

- Other aspects of the "purchaser's need": performance, safety, reliability, security, privacy, interfaces (and anything else that the purchaser may need)

Finally, 9000-3 asks that the supplier and purchaser cooperate during the development of the specification, via:

- Persons assigned the responsibility for establishing the spec

- Agreed-upon methods for reaching agreement on both original requirements and changes

- Use of well-defined terms and discussion of the background of certain requirements

- Review procedures for discussing the evolving specification

That is the extent of the direction given by 9000-3. But below the surface of the requirements specification task, there are many activities and issues that must be dealt with in attempting to meet 9000-3.

8.1.1 REQUIREMENTS ISSUES

The word "issue" is one of those wonderfully ambiguous English words that can mean so many things that it is difficult for it to mean anything in particular. My dictionary, for example, lists five definitions for "issue" as a noun, and then five more for its use as a verb.

However, there is one of those definitions that clearly represents what we want to discuss here. That definition of issue is:

"the point in question, an important topic for discussion"

This section of the material on requirements, section 8.1.1, is devoted to those issues, those important topics, that arise concerning the requirements life-cycle phase. There is a section like it for each of the additional topics of Chapter 8.

In those "issues" sections, it is our intent to present areas of controversy that have resisted resolution. That is, an issue raises strong differences of opinion, and no resolution of those differences has occurred to date. What that means is that "issues" represent areas of turbulence, and they also represent areas in which neither this nor any other book can offer a firm, definitive settlement. That is not to say, of course, that no resolution is possible. For each issue, there are in fact competing resolutions, each with its own advocates. But when the smoke of that advocacy has cleared away, there is simply no one clearly "correct" resolution. In many ways, the issues of software define the areas of greatest opportunity in the field, in that controversy and disagreement often lead to lively discussion, and, in the final analysis, clearer understanding.

In each of these "life-cycle" topics of this chapter, there will be lively issues to be dealt with. (Remember, we will present them, but we will not resolve them!) The requirements life-cycle phase is no exception.

The requirements issues have to do with the content and form of the requirements specification.

8.1.1.1 Content

Regarding content, there is some controversy in the software field over the need for a complete and unambiguous specification. Since 9000-3 requires such a specification, those organizations and projects wishing to conform have no choice but to follow its directives. But for the sake of completeness, it is worth stating the case for the opposite of "complete and unambiguous" requirements.

If one defines the most common problems encountered by troubled software projects, "requirements stability" is either at the top of or high up on most such lists. Requirements stability refers to the situation where, during the course of project implementation, there is some pressure on the part of the purchaser or customer to change the requirements. Obviously, having a "complete and unambiguous" specification is one way to take control of this problem. But in the minds of some software experts, that is an unrealistic way to gain such control.

The reason for this apparently contrarian viewpoint is that software is the chosen way of solving problems precisely because it is a malleable, and therefore changeable, product. (There is a reason why it is called "soft" ware!) It is not a weakness of the software field that maintenance activities consume 50–80% of most software project budgets over time, it is a strength. Software is the product that can evolve with the needs of its users over time. Studies show that roughly 60% of this high level of maintenance activity is involved with customer-defined changes (called "enhancements") to the software product.

Traditionally, software people have reacted to the need for change during the development process precisely as 9000-3 suggests: attempting to produce complete and unambiguous specifications, and then rigidly controlling their use. But given the evolutionary nature of the software product, some are beginning to call for software specifications that provide for evolution even as the product is being developed, if the customer understands and takes responsibility for a realistic incremental cost and schedule impact of the change. One book on the subject of software acquisition [Tardy 1991] takes the position that "many problems associated with software acquisitions are the consequence of a refusal to acknowledge the volatile nature of software requirements and to define acquisition strategies that take this into consideration." The author goes on to suggest that "the software acquisition manager must estimate the stability of the mandated requirements and plan for modifications in his strategy. He must be aware of the areas...where binding precision is unattainable or unproductive to avoid wasting effort in achieving a specification whose level of precision is unusable. He must design his acquisition strategy so that agents interpret imprecise requirements in an acceptable way." The author, confronting the 9000-3 requirement for "complete and unambiguous" specifications head on, says, "The first objective of the acquisition strategy was initially stated as: produce complete specifications. In view of the realities of software acquisition, this objective must be restated: effectively acquire a software product from unstable and imprecise requirements."

Another author on software engineering takes a similar point of view. In two different places, [Blum 1993 and 1995], Bruce Blum takes a position even more radical than that of the previous author. In the first reference, he says that "the days of 'give me a specification and I'll give you a debugged program' are gone forever." In the latter, he becomes more specific, anticipating a time when not just requirements, but software design as well, are subject to variation not just during development but during maintenance: "I see a 'new era of design' in which designing is integrated with doing, in which the designing is the doing ... Computing provides a mechanism ... that moves us from the plan-and-build paradigm to the build-and-evolve paradigm ... Production will consider design change a process-control variable."

Certainly 9000-3 has its heart in the right place on the subject of the content of the requirements specification. It is hard to argue against the need for "complete and unambiguous" requirements specifications. And yet, as we have seen, just such a case has been made, and it is difficult to argue against the logic of those who have made it. One journal, using excerpts from the work of the two authors mentioned above, even published a "special section on Requirements Specifications Considered Harmful" [SP 1993]!! Some developers actually plan a modification step after initial delivery in order to accommodate changes to requirements occurring during development.

Thus, we begin to see that meeting the apparently simple and straightforward requirements of 9000-3 in the area of requirements specifications is problematic, and at the same time crucial to the success of a software project. We will address the topic of how to resolve these difficulties later in this book.

8.1.1.2 Form

If meeting the content requirements of 9000-3 with respect to the requirements specification is problematic, the choice of form is even more problematic! There is an issue at the heart of present-day computer science regarding what form to choose for this specification—a formal mathematical one, or an informal natural-language one.

This issue is found under the computer science topic "formal methods." At the heart of the notion of formal methods is the belief that the requirements specification can only be "complete and unambiguous" if it is stated in a formal, mathematical language. Many such candidate languages have been advocated in many places (see, for example, three simultaneously orchestrated special issues of three leading computer science journals [Computer 1990, Software 1990, Transactions 1990]). But once again there is some controversy over the desirability of using such languages.

The issue of content, raised above, is obviously part of that controversy. If the requirements specification is to evolve over time to match the needs of the user, and if it is to be tolerant of unstable and imprecise requirements, then the extra cost needed to produce a stable, precise, and unambiguous specification clearly comes into question. (There is little data regarding the costs and benefits of formal specification techniques in practice because they are, to date, little used; but most experts would agree that their use will add at least up-front cost to the software development process, because they are more costly to construct.) If one accepts the 9000-3 call for complete and unambiguous specifications, then one must consider the value of formal specifications. If one accepts the contrarian view of the two authors above, then the need for formal specifications is at best considerably diminished (and, perhaps, obliterated!).

But the issue of form is more complicated than simply using the borrowed issue of content. It is important, in considering the form of the requirements specification, to consider who its target audience is. Certainly, the communication needs of its users must be taken into account in defining the form of any document, including this specification.

The target audience for a requirements specification is threefold (see, for example, [Davis 1989]):

- It is used by the designers to produce a design in conformance with the requirements it states.

- It is used by the customers and users to ensure that it states the requirements they want satisfied in the product being built.

- It is used by the testers to define requirements-driven test cases.

Let us characterize those target audiences. The first and third, the designers and testers, are presumably computer-knowledgeable specialists who are familiar with most of the candidate forms for all computing documentation. If a formal specification approach is used, for example, then (with appropriate training) the designers and testers can work with it.

But the second member of the target audience is more problematic. The customers and users of the product, presumably experts in their application domain, are not and should not have to be conversant with specialized languages used for software problem-solving. And certainly the formal specification language, as defined by computer scientists, requires its readers to be comfortable with mathematics and to engage in a specialized learning experience. Here, the formal specification language becomes not a help in defining complete and unambiguous requirements, but rather a barrier. If the customer/user cannot easily read the specification, then it does not serve as an effective vehicle to communicate proposed requirements between the supplier and the purchaser. Note that the 9000-3 terminology, in referring to this as the "purchaser's requirements specification," makes it extremely unlikely that formal languages could satisfy this need, since purchasers are unlikely to wish to use such exotic language forms. But notice further that the alternative, the use of natural language to express specifications, is well known to present ambiguity problems. Once again, conforming with the apparently simple needs of 9000-3 is fraught with complications beneath the surface.

We will address ways of overcoming these complications in the next section of this book.

References

[Blum 1993] Bruce I. Blum, "Talk About TEDIUM," *The Software Practitioner*, March 1993.

[Blum 1995] Bruce I. Blum, *Beyond Programming,* Oxford Press, 1995.

[Computer 1990] Special issue of *IEEE Computer* on "Formal Methods - Prelude to Virtuoso Software," Sept. 1990.

[Davis 1989] Alan M. Davis, *Software Requirements: Analysis and Specification*, Englewood Cliffs, N.J.: Prentice Hall, 1989.

[Software 1990] Special issue of *IEEE Software* on "Formal Methods— Developing Virtuoso Software," Sept. 1990.

[SP 1993] *The Software Practitioner*, special section on "Requirements Specifications Considered Harmful," March 1993.

[Tardy 1991] Jean E. Tardy, *A Map for Software Acquisition*, Monterege Design Inc., 1991.

[Transactions 1990] Special issue of *IEEE Transactions on Software Engineering* on "Formal Methods," Sept. 1990.

8.1.2 PROBLEM ANALYSIS

Now that the issues of the requirements phase have been discussed (if not dealt with!), let's look at those requirements processes that can help build a quality software product.

Problem analysis is a task performed on all software projects. *How* it is performed is subject to project-specific choices.

Problem analysis is that portion of the requirements task in which the systems analyst comes to understand the problem. Criteria for successful problem analysis, as noted in [Davis 1989], are:

- The result facilitates communication between the person with the problem and the problem-solver.

- It provides a means of defining system boundaries.

- It supports the notions of partitioning, abstraction, and projection (see below).

- It guides the problem solver toward the problem, not toward the solution.

- It allows for an examination of alternatives.

- It identifies conflicting alternatives where possible.

Problem analysis includes a problem identification phase and a problem decomposition phase. The identification phase is that portion in which an initial understanding of the problem is obtained. Possible starting places for problem identification are:

- **Inputs/outputs.** This is especially appropriate for small projects, and for applications dominated by input/output, such as transaction processing business applications.

- **Major functions.** This is especially appropriate for applications that are function-dominated, such as scientific applications.

- **Objects.** Object-oriented analysis is claimed to be the newly appropriate approach for all applications, but there is little evidence to support that claim. One would suspect that it is most appropriate for applications that manipulate objects, such as graphical user interface front ends. There is some initial evidence that, although real-time applications often manipulate objects, there are sufficient performance penalties to real-time solutions that object-oriented analysis and design may not be appropriate for those types of projects. Clearly, much more evaluative research is needed here.

- **Users**. This is especially appropriate for applications that have multiple users with differing needs, which is often a characteristic of large-scale business applications, such as management information systems.

- **Environment**. This is especially appropriate for applications that interact with a complex or demanding environment, such as real-time applications (especially embedded ones).

Problem decomposition builds on the problem identification phase by chopping the (presumably) large problem into smaller ones. Possible approaches are:

- **Abstraction**. This is a top-down process in which the essence of the problem at a high level is identified; then that essence is broken down into lower levels, each of which is more detailed, specific, and concrete than that from which it was decomposed; and the whole process is repeated until the problem is grasped.

- **Partitioning**. This is a bottom-up process in which a difficult-to-grasp whole problem is partitioned into a set of smaller problems, each of which is similarly decomposed. The totality of the requirements for the overall problem is then the sum of the requirements for the smaller problems.

- **Projection**. This is a multiviewed process in which the problem is examined from the points of view of the key players in the eventual solution (e.g., the users). The totality of the requirements of the overall problem is then the sum of the requirements from each key player projection.

For what project types are these approaches most useful? Abstraction is probably the default approach if neither of the others is superior. Partitioning is most useful when it seems impossible to grasp the total problem; that would be characteristic of very large and complex projects (or perhaps innovative projects). Projection is useful for projects where the views of the key players vary enormously; as pointed out before, this is characteristic of many large business applications, especially management information systems.

Reference

[Davis 1989] Alan M. Davis, *Software Requirements: Analysis and Specifications,* Englewood Cliffs, N.J.: Prentice Hall, 1989. (Much of the material in this section, and some from the next, is derived from Davis' work.)

8.1.3 MODELING AND SIMULATION

Often the process of understanding problems is so complicated that purely mental approaches are insufficient. For problems that are complex, it may be necessary to build a model of the problem and then construct a simulation to execute the model under various circumstances in order to explore its behavior.

Fortunately, there are software-based approaches to support modeling and simulation. There are off-the-shelf modeling/simulation packages that make it easy to represent standard kinds of system elements so that a simulation can be constructed relatively cheaply and easily. There are also modeling/simulation languages, in which the problem analyzer may construct a specialized model of the problem at hand, and run simulations based on general-purpose simulation facilities in the language.

For what types of projects are modeling and simulation most appropriate? First of all, for those that are very large; second, for those with a great number of complex interfaces; third, for those with difficult-to-achieve performance requirements; and fourth, for those that are unlike any problem ever tackled before. Thus, modeling and simulation should be considered on large projects, on real-time projects, and on innovative projects.

8.1.4 PROTOTYPING

Prototyping is the construction of a proposed problem solution in order to see whether it will be effective. Although the distinction between modeling and prototyping is not crisp, modeling tends to be about the problem, whereas prototyping tends to be about the solution.

Prototyping may be used in both the requirements and design phases of software. In either phase, its goal is to explore a key element in the eventual construction of a working system. In the requirements phase, it is used to study the understanding of a key aspect or all of the problem in order to explore the feasibility and usefulness of solution options. For example, a common use of prototyping is to build a working user interface in order to see if it matches the needs of the users. In fact, there are generalized tools available in the marketplace to do precisely this, so that user interface prototyping often need not involve programming.

More commonly, however, the prototype is a working program, a subset of the eventual solution, often programmed with little consideration of product quality since its purpose is exploratory and the intention is to discard it when it has served its purpose. Requirements prototypes, in addition to exploring user interfaces, may explore timing requirements to see if a solution is feasible; functionality needs, to see if any are in conflict; object definitions, to see what may be reused and what is not available; and so on. Design prototypes may explore proposed solutions in order to see if they are programmable and/or will satisfy the stated requirements.

The biggest issues with prototyping are twofold:

- All too often there is management pressure to evolve the prototype into the working final product (the term "rapid prototyping" reflects this school of thought). There are times when this is appropriate; but recall that prototypes are usually hurriedly thrown together without quality considerations to explore a particular problem. As such, they are often poor candidates for a high-quality final solution.

- It is very difficult to estimate projects where prototyping is necessary. The construction and execution of a prototype system often has cost and schedule impacts, and the decisions made following examination of prototype results may change the course of the project. The net result may be faster software construction overall because of a better understanding of the requirements, but "rapid prototyping" is probably initially not rapid at all!

(Note that these issues are part of two broader management issues in software: in the current management approach, too much emphasis is put on schedule conformance and too little on quality; and estimates are often required before the problem is sufficiently well understood to make the estimate meaningful.)

For what types of problems is prototyping most appropriate? First, for those that are innovative. It may well be unclear whether a solution is possible until one or a series of prototypes is constructed. Second, for those that are very large. Prototyping is a way of elaborating the problem decomposition in order to better grasp what is being tackled. It is less clear whether prototyping is appropriate for particular domains (large real-time problems may prototype to check performance requirements) or for particularly critical projects.

8.1.5 REPRESENTATION

This is the issue dealt with earlier in the Requirements Issues section. What we saw there is that there is some con-

troversy over the need for rigorous, unambiguous requirements specifications, and over the formality of the language
used to write the specifications.

There are perhaps eight choices for the representation
used to write the requirements specification:

- Natural language

- Structured English (constrained to a problem- or
  requirements-specific vocabulary)

- Formal language

- Decision tables

- Finite state machine

- Data structure model

- Dataflow model

- Data dictionary

These representations may be mixed and matched. For
example, it is common in some contemporary applications
to mix natural language, dataflow models, and a data dictionary.

It is important to note that CASE (computer-aided software engineering) tools exist to assist in the creation and
maintenance of most of these representations. Since the creation and maintenance of requirements representation is a
cumbersome, largely clerical job, such CASE tools are very
helpful. (They are not, however, the breakthrough support
that many originally claimed them to be.)

For which types of projects are these representations
most appropriate? Natural language is still the representation of choice when customers and users must understand
the specification. In general, that need exists for almost all
projects. Structured English may substitute for it, as long as
the language is carefully chosen to be customer-/user-read-
able. Formal specification languages are rarely useful,

although they are required by law for certain types of military real-time systems in England! Decision tables may be useful for projects with a great number of logical choices, such as certain kinds of management information (business) applications. There is currently exploration underway to determine whether they are the representation of choice for business-rules-based business applications. (There is some concern as to how well decision tables scale up to large problems, however.) Finite state machines are often useful for real-time applications, where the problem is often about various states of switching devices. Data structure, flow, and dictionary approaches are extremely useful for business applications, although some have found them useful for other applications as well. Aside from applications, there is little to choose among these representations on the basis of project size, criticality, or innovativeness.

8.1.6 TRACEABILITY

Given that the requirements are the platform upon which the whole problem solution is based, wouldn't it be nice if it were possible to identify, for each portion of the eventual as-built program, those requirements that it was coded to satisfy? Wouldn't it be nice, given a particular requirement, to find all portions of the code that were built to satisfy it?

That's what traceability is all about. The concept of traceability is that there will be bidirectional links between the problem requirements and all the components of the as-built problem solution—the design, the code, the test cases, even the documentation. In theory, traceability could be enormously important to the software construction and maintenance processes. But that theory has not, to date, been borne out in practice.

It has not been for lack of trying. There are traceability requirements in the U.S. Department of Defense requirements for building software. There are traceability CASE tools on the market to help deliver on the DoD requirements. Some software houses have been using pieces of the traceability approach for over 20 years now. But the fact of the matter is, the realities of the theory have been nearly impossible to achieve.

The problem is that there is many a slip between the problem requirements and the as-built solution. Most prominent in those slips is the so-called "requirements explosion"— as an evolving software product moves from requirements definition to designed solution, the original problem requirements have "exploded" into the collection of implied design requirements necessary to build a solution to the problem. Some have measured that explosion to be two or more orders of magnitude (that is, the explosion is a factor of 100 or more). Furthermore, as the software product evolves, pieces of design and code are created to satisfy not just one but several of those explicit and implicit requirements. Thus, requirements not only explode, they entangle. Good modular programs may contain modules, for example, that help solve the problem stated by a dozen or more requirements.

This is, of course, precisely the kind of problem that software can help us solve. That is, returning to theory once more, it should be possible to build a comprehensive CASE tool that damps out the explosion and unsnarls the tangle. Perhaps that tool is even on the marketplace horizon. In other words, don't give up on a solution to the traceability problem. Help may be coming.

But in the meantime, it is difficult to recommend full-fledged traceability except in those projects where it is required (DoD real-time embedded applications). However, one limited form of traceability is possible and commonly achieved: linking requirements to test cases. There, a matrix is constructed to show which test cases exercise which requirements. That is easy to do either manually or with the help of tools, and we recommend here that all types of projects employ this technology, regardless of size, application domain, criticality, or innovativeness.

8.1.7 REVIEW

Reviews have been consistently shown to be the most effective and cost-effective way of removing errors from the software product. The data to support that statement is generally found in studies about design and code reviews, but there is every reason to believe that requirements reviews are just as important.

The purpose of the requirements review is to gather the players in the requirements process around the requirements specification, with the expectation that the gathering will lead to specification buy-in. The gathering may be literal (in the form of a meeting) or figurative (in the form of independent and separate review). The process may be formal (with well-defined review rules and assignments) or informal ("please read the spec and tell us of any errors you find"). The key players are the customers, users, and systems analysts who created the specification, and whatever levels of their management are appropriate. Note that because the key players include non-computing knowledgeable participants, this review is among the least computing-technical of the reviews held during the software process. That is not surprising, of course, since the whole requirements process should be focused on the problem to be solved, not its solution.

For what kinds of projects should requirements reviews be held? For just about all (very small projects might be the exception). Since there are varying degrees of formality implied by the heading "review," as we have defined it, there is virtually no reason not to hold at least an informal requirements review on the least significant project. Formality should increase as we move toward large projects, or critical projects. (Care should be exercised here. It is clear that *rigorous* reviews are what is really important, where rigor implies a focused, conscientious, and skilled concentration on the review product at hand. Whether *formal* reviews [based, again, on rules] tend to be more rigorous has not been proven or disproven.) The nature of the innovative project will determine the degree of formality needed for that type of project—if the innovation is about the problem, those who understand the problem best (the customers/users) should clearly participate in a fairly formal review process; if the innovation is about the solution approach, the need for formality is diminished.

The need for requirements reviews is fairly application-independent as well. For business applications with a varied set of customers/users, the need is particularly acute. For systems programs, where the software developers may be their own best customers, the need is considerably diminished. But otherwise it is safe to say that all application domains can make good use of requirements reviews.

8.1.8 REQUIREMENTS SUMMARY

At the beginning of this section, we presented the 9000-3 requirements for the requirements phase of software development. They had to do with ensuring that:

- Functional requirements were complete and unambiguous.

- All other requirements (e.g., performance, safety, etc.) were covered.

- Responsibilities were assigned, and conditions of agreement and terms were defined.

- Review procedures were provided.

What we see here immediately is that the requirements for building quality software go far beyond the requirements of ISO 9000. That is, ISO is a necessary, but not sufficient, statement of things that must be done to ensure quality software.

In one sense, that is a positive finding. It should not be difficult to meet the stated goals of ISO 9000, since they are not terribly taxing. In another sense, it is a disturbing finding. It means that enterprises conforming with ISO 9000 can still do a very bad job of building quality software.

There is, to be sure, some correlation between what 9000-3 demands and the techniques we have listed. The goals of the sections on problem analysis, modeling and simulation, prototyping, and representation are certainly in sync with the 9000-3 goal of preparing complete and unambiguous requirements specifications that list *all* customer requirements. The material on traceability, among other things, is a way of ensuring that the requirements are complete. The section on reviews responds explicitly to the 9000-3 requirement for "review procedures." An examination of these differences suggests that the intent of 9000-3 may be to state *what* is to be done to ensure quality, without specifying *how* it is to be achieved. But the distance between "what" and "how," especially in the requirements phase of software development, is enormous. And, as we have seen, as we study the "how," we begin to see cracks in the facade of the "what." For example, some projects may achieve a complete and unambiguous definition of input/output or object-oriented rather than functional requirements; or certain kinds of projects—small and uncritical, or innovative, for example—may require less than "complete and unambiguous" specifications.

Table 8.1 below summarizes, by project type, what "how" approaches should supplement (or, occasionally, replace) the 9000-3 "what" for various types of projects.

Note that large and critical projects should use most of the techniques and tools listed, and that small and uncritical projects need fewer of them. Note also that for some techniques and tools, application is the best determiner of appropriateness, but for others size and criticality are.

One final comment. The entries in Table 8.1 are subject to legitimate disagreement. Advocates of particular techniques and tools may believe, for example, that their concept should be used on all projects, regardless of type. We believe most strongly that those advocates are almost always wrong.

But at the same time, we believe that the content of Table 8.1 should be treated as recommendations, not as hard and fast rules, and that the experience and wisdom of project participants may (and on some occasions should) overrule these suggestions.

Table 8.1 Project Types vs. Techniques: Requirements

Technique/ Tool	Size		Application				Criticality		Innova-tiveness	
	Lg	Sm	Bus	Sci	Sys	R-T	High	Low	High	Low
Problem Analysis	U	IO	IO, U	F	O? F	E	See applic.		See applic.	
Modeling and Simulation	Y	N	P	P	P	Y	Y	P	P	P
Prototyping	P	N	P	N	P	P	Y	P	Y	P
Representation	See applic.		Na SE DT D3	?	Na FL DT	Na SE FL FS	See applic.		See applic.	
Traceability	TC	TC	WP	WP	WP	Y	Y	WP	WP	WP
Review	Y	?	Y	Y	?	Y	Y	?	Y	?

Legend:
Problem Analysis starting places:
E = Environment
F = Function
IO= Input/Output
O = Object
O?= Object if appropriate
U = Users
See Applic. = Choice here should depend on application selection

Modeling and Simulation, Prototyping:
N = No, or usually not
P = Perhaps, depending on other circumstances
Y = Yes, or often

Representation:
Na = Natural Language
SE = Structured English
FL = Formal Language
FS = Finite State Machine
DT = Decision Tables
D3 = Data Structure, Dataflow, and Data Dictionary
See applic. = Choice here should depend on application
? = There is no clear choice

Traceability:
TC = At least for test cases
WP = Whenever Possible, test cases + all artifacts
N = No

Review:
Y = Yes
? = Depends on circumstances

8.2 DESIGN AND IMPLEMENTATION

The gap between what ISO 9000-3 demands and what good software practice demands begins to grow significantly in the design and implementation phases of software development.

The requirements of ISO 9000-3 for software design are relatively straightforward:

- The activities should be carried out in a disciplined manner.

- Input and output should be specified, and design rules and internal interface definitions should be "examined."

- A systematic design methodology "appropriate to the type of software product being developed" should be used (the quoted material is an interesting acknowledgment by 9000-3 that design approaches must be application-specific).

- Past design lessons learned should be used, and past mistakes avoided.

- Product design should facilitate testing, maintenance, and use.

- The product of the design phase should be subject to review.

It is hard to argue with any of these requirements for design. The requirement that design "be carried out in a disciplined manner," which could be interpreted to nullify the importance of creativity in the design process, is actually (and specifically) about producing a design that correctly satisfies the specification rather than deferring establishing correctness to the testing and validation phases. The methodology requirement is sufficiently open-ended that almost anything will be acceptable. The notions that design should benefit from lessons learned and should facilitate testing are, at least conceptually, universally accepted.

However, as anyone who designs software will quickly recognize, this open-endedness does not provide sufficient guidance to the design process to guarantee the quality for which 9000-3 is striving. Another level of design guidance must be present in a project's quality approach. The remainder of this section is about that additional guidance.

The same thing is true of implementation. (Note that "implementation," in 9000-3, clearly refers to the process of coding the design, producing the test-ready product. Unfortunately, in computing circles the term is ambiguous. Information systems people tend to use "implementation" to mean "making the product ready for use." That is not the use of the term in 9000-3 and in this book. If that difference in definition bothers you, whenever you see the word "implementation," think "coding.") The guidance provided by 9000-3 on the implementation process is rudimentary—necessary, but not sufficient:

- The activities should be carried out in a disciplined manner.

- Rules and standards (e.g., coding standards, language choice) should be specified and observed.

- Methods and tools should be "appropriate" to satisfying purchaser requirements.

- The product of the coding phase should be subject to review.

As with the design requirements of 9000-3, the implementation requirements are insufficient to provide guidance for coders. Once again, it is the purpose of this section of this book to provide the additional level of detail needed to allow the creation of a meaningful and useful project quality system.

The sections that follow will deal with specific design and implementation approaches, and the criteria for choosing among them for a particular project. But first, let us examine the issues that effect the application of 9000-3 to design and implementation.

8.2.1 DESIGN AND IMPLEMENTATION ISSUES

Much remains to be learned about the process of design in general, and software design in particular. That lack of knowledge forms the basis for the issues that surround software design.

Regarding implementation, the number of issues is much smaller. The process of coding, although a complex activity, is sufficiently well understood that it leaves far fewer issues to be dealt with.

8.2.1.1 Cognitive Design

Textbooks on design often show it as a process subject to methodological approaches, one where the application of the appropriate methodology will allow the designer to produce an effective, efficient design. Once the design is produced, the textbooks say, the designer may document it in some form of representation. The essence of those textbooks, then, is the notion that design is a combination of methodology and representation.

But the implication of this textbook approach is that design is a mechanistic, controllable process. Common sense and lots of experience in lots of design fields tells us, to the contrary, that it is not. What is missing from this methodology + representation picture of design?

It is the cognitive process, the role of the creative mind, that is missing from the mechanistic picture of design. Studies have shown that the essence of design is a heuristic, iterative, and in fact opportunistic process, involving a great deal of mental modeling and mental simulation before a design can be obtained. The textbook methodological approach may steer us in the proper directions, and the textbook representation techniques may give us effective ways of documenting the result of the design process, but the essence of design is a series of mental steps that lend themselves little, if at all, to mechanistic processes.

Earlier we said that design is heuristic, iterative, and opportunistic. What did we mean by that? And why do we believe it is true?

A number of key empirical studies of the design process were conducted in the late 1980s (e.g., [Adelson 1984], [Curtis 1987]), and their results were consistent and clear. Skilled designers, studied in the act of designing, used approaches that were:

- **Heuristic and iterative**—The designers, using heuristic (trial and error) processes, constructed a mental model of a proposed design solution, executed mental simulations of that model using mentally generated test data (to see if the model would solve the problem), and refined the mental model by successive iterations until it was sufficient to solve the problem at hand.

- **Opportunistic**—The designers, instead of following a careful and disciplined top-down procedure, as the "experts" in the field of design advocated, actually allowed their minds to leap from one design issue to apparently unconnected other design issues during the act of completing a design.

The findings of those studies, although controversial at first (especially in the world of computing theory—practitioners were much less surprised by the findings), have begun to earn respectability in the mainstream of computer science. The fact that cognition and creativity are at the heart of the design process does not, of course, diminish the importance of methodology and representation. But it does suggest that merely learning a methodology and a collection of representations does not a good designer make.

It is this issue that requires some interpretation of the "discipline" requirements of 9000-3. As we have previously mentioned, as long as the requirement for discipline in 9000-3 is used to imply that the result of the design process should be complete and correct, not intentionally deferring the removal of design errors to a later life-cycle phase, there is no problem with it. If, however, the phrase is interpreted to mean that design should be a highly controlled, mechanistic process, then that interpretation of 9000-3 will surely lead to the opposite of the spirit of the standard, designs that are ineffective and—in the end result—lack quality.

8.2.1.2 The Beginning and Ending of Design

Precisely because we know that the process of design is not mechanistic, but rather cognitive, software professionals try to start the design process with established, "used" design models. It is much more efficient—and much less error-prone, in general—to begin that mental modeling and simulation described in the previous section with the model of a solution previously employed on some similar problem.

Whereas starting a design process from scratch means beginning the design process with a fairly simple model, and continually adding layers of complexity in order to respond to the complexities of the problem at hand (the image of unpeeling an onion comes to mind!), it is much more effective to start with an established design model and modify it during the simulation process in order to solve the stated problem. Thus, well before the term "reuse" became popular in the computer science theory world, designers have been reusing designs (as well as coded modules) in their work. Several research findings [Lammers 1986, Visser 1987] have substantiated this fact. One researcher stated that "designers seldom start from scratch," and other researchers report designers themselves making similar statements in interview sessions.

Because of this, the best designers tend to be those with the richest store of past working designs in their repertoire. It is almost as if top designers have backpacks full of designs from which they draw candidate initial designs when a new problem is encountered.

If the beginning of design involves a mixture of methodology and analogy, as we have just seen, then the textbook view is clearly simplistic. But the ending of design is in many ways even less like the textbooks portray it. The typical textbook picture of the way to end design, and switch to coding, is to do so when the design has reached the level at which a competent programmer can understand and complete it. But appealing as that notion is, there is many a slip twixt that "competent programmer" theory and reality.

Most attempts to flesh out what exists at that ending-of-design point come to the conclusion that the design is stated in a collection of "primitives," subproblems that any competent programmer will know how to code. In a simplistic sense, that view is correct. But in the real world, it just doesn't work that way.

The reason it doesn't is that all software people differ in their capabilities, due to both innate individual differences

(differences of up to 30-1 have been reported; that is some software people are sometimes 30 times as effective as others) and personal experiences. What is a primitive to one person will remain a complex problem to another. Thus, a designer who hands off a high-level primitive to a coder who does not share that primitive will find the coder doing considerably more design before coding can begin; and the designer who hands off an overly elaborate primitive to a more sophisticated coder whose primitives are at a higher level will find the coder scrapping portions of the design and redoing them. In fact, there is nothing wrong with either of those occurrences, given a mismatch between the primitives of designer and coder (and such a mismatch is almost inevitable).

It is important to note that these primitive differences cannot, in all likelihood, be trained away. If I am an expert in report generation program design and code, and I hand off a report generation design to a coder who is an expert in compiler design, there will be a mismatch. And if the roles of designer and coder are reversed, there will still be a mismatch. To train away these primitive differences would require smoothing out both innate and experiential individual differences, and that is simply unlikely to happen, no matter how effective the training program.

Thus, the ending of design—the handing off of design to coder—will always be problematic.

✳ 8.2.1.3 Implementation Standards

Implementation standards are a vital part of the software design and, probably more important, coding processes. If program pieces created by different people are to fit together (in all the meanings of the word "fit"), then there must be predictability to those program pieces, and standards are the way to achieve that predictability.

Given that, why are standards an issue? The reason is that even though standards are important, they are given too much importance in some views of the software process.

For example, just because some standards are goodness, more standards are not betterness. There comes a point at which profuse standards, too numerous to remember and/or enforce, are simply ignored. The problem of too many standards is essentially equivalent to the problem of too few standards: the desired goal of predictability is not achieved.

There is another problem with standards. Among software-ignorant quality assurance people, there is all too often a belief that adherence to standards is the same as achievement of quality. In this circle of believers, the purpose of design and coding reviews is to check conformance to standards, and only to check conformance to standards. That view is, of course, extremely dangerous. A standards-conforming program may still be unreliable, inefficient, unmaintainable, and in fact out of sync with most of the attributes of quality. Having said that, it is important to note that standards, once defined and documented, must be enforced. (Why else have them?!) Ensuring standards conformance is simply one part of the review process, but it is not at all the most important part.

8.2.1.4 Automatic Generation of Code

It has been popular in the world of computing theory to predict that code generators will be created to remove the necessity of a coding phase at all. The software engineer, in this view, will write the specifications, and a tool of some sort will convert the specifications into code automatically.

For the most part, this prediction has not come true, and there are many who take the position that it is unlikely to. There are several problems with that viewpoint. The first is that it is not clear, in this context, what the theorists mean by "specifications." Although, in general, the word is taken to mean requirements specification—and who among us would not like to see the capability to automatically generate a software solution from a problem statement!—in fact, an examination of the automatic generation research literature will show that these specifications often turn out to really be designs, often at a fairly detailed level. Certainly, if the definition of "specifications" is bent far enough toward code, it is possible to automate the generation of code from this kind of specification! But in saying that, we have said very little.

Another problem with the automatic generation of code is that such tools must understand a great deal about both programming and the application domain of the problem to be solved. That is a huge requirement for such a tool. However, it also provides us with a clue as to how future progress may be made in the creation of such tools. If an application domain becomes sufficiently well understood, so the writing of code for that kind of application can, for a human, become somewhat mechanistic, then the creation of an automatic code generation tool does indeed become possible. As early as the 1960s, for example, the programming language RPG (Report Program Generator) was an instantiation of such an automatic code generator for the database/file-extraction, report-generation domain. Modern-day 4GLs are elaborations and refinements of that early work.

Progress in our ability to automatically generate code hinges, then, on our ability to mechanize problem solutions in well-understood application domains. Because of that, such progress will be slow. Today's 9000-3 student should not expect automatic code generation to be today's or tomorrow's way to build quality software. But in another couple of decades? Who can predict that far ahead?

References

[Adelson 1984] Beth Adelson and Elliot Soloway, "A Model of Software Design," Yale University Department of Computer Science, Oct. 1984.

[Curtis 1987] Bill Curtis, Raymonde Guindon, Herb Krasner, Diane Walz, Joyce Elam, and Neil Iscoe, "Empirical Studies of the Design Process: Papers for the Second Workshop on Empirical Studies of Programmers," MCC Technical Report Number STP-260-87, 1987.

[Lammers 1986] Susan Lammers, *Programmers at Work*, Redmond, WA: Microsoft Press, 1986.

[Visser 1987] Willemien Visser, "Strategies in Programming Programmable Controllers: A Field Study on a Professional Programmer," *Proceedings of the Second Empirical Studies of Programmers Conference*, Ablex, 1987.

8.2.2 PROCESS, DATA, OBJECT, AND EVENT DESIGN

Process-oriented design is design focused on the functionality of the problem and its solution. Data-oriented design is focused on the data manipulated by the processes. Object-oriented design is focused on a blend of the two, attaching to specific data objects the processes that can be performed on them. Event-oriented design is focused on events that occur and must be serviced during the execution of the solution.

There is considerable controversy among these four design approaches. The process approach is the oldest, and probably still has the most adherents in practice. The object approach is the newest, and probably has the most adherents in the world of theory. The data approach is also well established in practice, and has many adherents there (under the banner "information engineering," there are also adherents in the theory world). The event approach has more splintered backing, since it is generally acknowledged to be useful largely for real-time embedded problems. (More information about the first three approaches may be found in *Building Quality Software*. However, that book does not cover event-driven design. The references [Harel 1990] and [Sanden 1989] should help explain some fundamentals of that approach.)

Some take the position that the two fundamental approaches to design are those of process and data, and that objects and events are just ways of packaging process and data in different ways. There is certainly historic justification for taking that position, and it is possible to make a logical case for it as well.

Both process and data approaches are well supported by CASE tools, and there are a growing number of object-oriented CASE tools as well. Tools are available as well to support the event approach, but they are less well known [Harel 1990]. These tools are helpful in creating the design representation once the design is obtained.

It is interesting to note here that the advocates of the object-oriented approach claim significant advantages for it because of its "naturalness" and its ability to assist in reuse. The former claim has been at least tentatively refuted [Vessey 1994, Moynihan 1994], but the latter has a growing body of evidence supporting it (e.g., [Stark 1993]).

Let us examine the five project type dimensions and decide for which these respective approaches might be the most important. The most important thing to be said here is about the application. If the application is functionality-focused, then the process approach is most likely to address the key areas of the problem. If the application is data-focused, then that approach tends to be best. Similarly, the object and event approaches are best for applications characterized by the dominance of objects or events. Thus, the key dimension is the application domain—scientific and systems problems will, in general, be more compatible with the process approach. Business applications are more likely to find the data approach useful, since many of them focus heavily on data. Real-time applications will be best served by the event approach. (There are exceptions here, of course—systems program applications in the area of graphical user interfaces find the object approach far more useful, and it may well be that, with more experience in the application of object approaches to business problems, we will find the object approach more useful. Much remains to be learned in the application of methods and tools on an application-focused basis.)

Regarding project size, there is little basis for choosing among the three approaches. Small projects are no more likely to require a particular approach than large ones. It is important to note, however, that if a project is one of a family of similar projects (and in that sense part of a large project), the object-oriented approach and its reuse benefits may be best.

Regarding project criticality, again, there is little basis for choice. Following the needs of the application domain is the most likely way to successfully respond to project criticality needs.

Regarding project innovativeness, once again, the choice of domain is still probably the dominant criteria. It is popular among theorists, as this is written, to suggest that the object-oriented approach is best for all problem solutions, and it is easy to imagine that it is the current design approach of choice among those tackling innovative problems. However, there is no data at present to suggest that innovative problems are better (or worse) solved using object-oriented approaches.

References

[Harel 1990] D. Harel, "Statecharts, a Visual Approach to Complex Systems," *Scientific Computer Programming*, 1990.

[Moynihan 1994] Tony Moynihan, "An Experimental Comparison of Object-Oriented and Functional Decomposition as Paradigms for Communicating System Functionality to Users," *Proceedings of the Fourth International Conference on Information Systems Development*, Bled, Slovenia, Sept. 20–22 1994.

[Sanden 1989] Bo Sanden, "An Entity-Life Modeling Approach to the Design of Concurrent Software," *Communications of the ACM*, March 1989.

[Stark 1993] Mike Stark, "Impacts of Object-Oriented Technologies: Seven Years of Software Engineering," *Journal of Systems and Software*, Nov. 1993.

[Vessey 1994] Iris Vessey and Sue A. Conger, "Requirements Specification: Learning Object, Process, and Data Methodologies," *Communications of the ACM*, May 1994.

8.2.3 TOP-DOWN, BOTTOM-UP, AND HARD-PART FIRST DESIGN

Regardless of whether the design approach is process-, data-, object-, or event-oriented, there is another overall choice to make in design approach: What parts of the design should be tackled first? Some say the answer is to proceed top-down, from the most important requirements to the least, expanding the evolving design solutions in a hierarchical manner. Others say design should proceed bottom-up, starting with reusable components and assembling them into a whole product. Still others say that, although each of those approaches makes sense in its own way, most practitioners actually use a third approach. Earlier, we characterized this third approach as "opportunistic"—designer minds dart about from one part of the design to another as they perceive problems arising that need to be addressed. In this section, we give the term "opportunistic" a bit more dignity, calling it instead "hard-part-first" design. In this viewpoint, the reason the mind is darting opportunistically from one part of the design to another is that it keeps encountering hard problems related to, but remote from, the current design problem being addressed, and it quickly leaps to those related problems because they are obstacles to be removed from the overall design process.

Because all the rationales for these three design approaches are all worthy, it would be preferable to approach design in such a way that the advantages of all three approaches could be maintained. For example, the top-down approach (it is the textbook-favored approach, as of this writing) has the advantage that it looks like a planned and organized approach. In fact, even in the midst of bottom-up and hard-part-first design, there is generally some sort of overall top-down plan that the reusable modules, or hard problems, fit into. Furthermore, David Parnas has said that all design approaches should "fake" a top-down approach (!), in the sense that the final design documentation should be written in top-down fashion regardless of the way the design was achieved, since top-down design is more understandable to someone trying to comprehend a design than the other two approaches [Parnas 1986]. (Imagine, for example, design documentation written in the order in which the design was accomplished by a hard-part-first designer. The documentation would appear to be disorganized and almost random, especially since one person's hard part may be another person's easy part!)

Bottom-up design has always been present in software, but it has come into more favor with the advent of object-oriented design and its emphasis on reusable objects. A good design approach must somehow manage to capture the advantages of reuse in the overall, perhaps top-down, design structure.

Hard-part-first design is seldom articulated but often practiced. Its opposite, easy-part-first design, is probably the most significantly wrong design approach of them all, since the early easy design solutions will often have to be discarded as it becomes obvious that they are incompatible with what is needed to solve the hard problems.

What we see here is that all three approaches—top-down, bottom-up, and hard-part-first—are essential elements of the design process. The good designer will find ways to utilize all three in almost all software projects. Probably this means constructing a rough-cut, top-down design first; then examining the available reusable components to determine which parts of the current problem have already been solved; and then addressing the hard parts of the top-down design. When the design is complete, its representation should be top-down in form.

What about the types of software projects? Should this advice be modified depending on project size, application domain, criticality, or innovativeness? The answer is, probably not. Projects that are large because there are many similar sub-projects will probably evolve many reusable components, and thus may be more bottom-up than average.

Projects that are innovative may have more than the usual number of hard parts, and thus may be more hard-part-first than average. But other than that, the advice above is good for all projects, regardless of their nature

Reference

[Parnas 1986] David L. Parnas, "A Rational Design Process: How and Why to Fake It," *IEEE Transactions on Software Engineering*, Feb. 1986.

8.2.4 REPRESENTATION

Once the design is obtained—by process, data, object, or event methods, and by a top-down, bottom-up, or hard-part-first approach—it must be written down in some sort of formal fashion. Of course, the evolving design is written down during the design process, but often that form of representation is informal and temporary. (Designs have been known to be written initially on napkins or tablecloths!) It is important to note two fundamentally different reasons for design representation: first, as an intellectual tool, to help the designer think about the design; and second, as a communication tool, to help the designer pass information on to the programmer or maintainer. The former can be informal and transient, but the latter must be formal and permanent.

There are a number of formal design representation techniques, nearly all of them supported by CASE tools to assist in their construction and maintenance. Dataflow diagrams, structure charts, and/or program design language (pseudocode) are among the most popular language forms. Representation CASE tools not only support most of these representational forms, but they also perform automated design checking (which will be discussed in a later section).

In this book, we will not spend much time (and space) on design representation techniques. They are well documented in many other sources, and by now most software professionals have been trained in one or more forms. (See, for example, such design representation summaries as [Tripp 1988] and [Webster 1988]). And, it is important to add, although representation is always important—good representation techniques can help clarify the thinking of the designer, often exposing errors not visible until the representation is done—representation is much less a key part of design than the approaches that we discussed earlier. That is why, for example, the design representation CASE tools have not produced the breakthrough that many claimed they would.

Also, because of the fact that representation is not key, the choice of representation for a specific project should usually be based not on the representation itself, but on the techniques chosen to perform the design. For example, a design that is driven by process and performed top-down will have a form of representation (and the related CASE tools) accompanying it. Similarly, data design ("information engineering") has a different representational technique. The bottom line of this section is, then, that the project type does not enter into the representation decision except through the choices that have already been made regarding process/data/object/event and top-down/bottom-up/hard-part-first.

References

[Tripp 1988] Leonard L. Tripp, "A Survey of Graphical Notations for Program Design - An Update," *ACM Software Engineering Notes*, Oct. 1988.
[Webster 1988] Dallas E. Webster, "Mapping the Design Information Representation Terrain," *IEEE Computer,* Dec. 1988.

8.2.5 FAULT-TOLERANT DESIGN

Although it is popular to exhort software people to produce error-free products, and some researchers claim they have found ways to achieve that, the fact of the matter is that software products—like all human-created products—will always have errors in them. No matter how many error-removal processes are used to address the problem, some errors always remain uncaught.

The trick is, of course, to make sure that any errors in the software have minimum impact on its ability to function. Later, in the section of this book on testing and validation, we will discuss ways of performing the best possible error removal. But here, we must address the issue of what the designer can do to ensure that any errors remaining have that minimal impact.

In traditional disciplines, this problem is addressed by designing redundant components. A component that may fail is replicated in such a way that if one instantiation of the component fails, another can leap in to replace it. The assumption is that multiple redundant components will not share the same failure characteristics.

In software, redundancy as traditionally practiced will not work. Since software neither breaks nor wears out, redundant software components will all share the same faults, and replacing a failed software component with its replication accomplishes nothing.

Software researchers and practitioners have addressed this problem with something called "diversity." The notion of redundancy is simulated in software by having extra code built to dynamically handle problems that slip through the error-removal nets. Sometimes this takes the form of having multiple design and implementation teams build replications of components of concern using entirely different approaches. The assumption here is that multiple design teams will not create the same faults as one another. (It is interesting to note the implications of this assumption—that given a problem to be solved in software, it is unlikely that multiple design teams will come up with the same design approach. This has profound implications for the field. It speaks of the immaturity of the field, but more important, it suggests that attempts by methodology and standardization to make the design of software products predictable are probably doomed, at least at this point in time.)

Given that diverse (rather than redundant) components are software's answer to fault tolerance, how do we glue those components together to achieve the product reliability desired? The answer is, there are three approaches:

- The use of recovery blocks, sections of extra (diverse) code whose task is to dynamically accommodate and recover from whatever problem has occurred

- The use of N-version programming, where the multiple design teams described above solve the same critical problem and the software dynamically switches from one version to another as one version is found to be failing

- The use of data diversity, where key data is protected through replication and dynamic switchover mechanisms

Fault-tolerant software is still, to a large extent, at the research and development stage. That is, there are few applications of fault tolerance in practice (the aerospace and rail industries are exceptions). Rigorous use of contemporary error removal techniques is still the mode of operation for most software projects.

That brings us to the matter of the types of projects on which fault-tolerance techniques should be used. Here, the answer is easy. Critical projects deserve all the help they can get in running error-free. That is why the aerospace and rail industries, as noted above, use the techniques now, and have been using them for two or more decades. For most other projects, the cost and complexity of fault-tolerant approaches are an unnecessary addition. Specifically, there is no more reason to use fault-tolerant approaches on large projects than on small ones (or vice versa); application domain matters little in the choice to use fault-tolerant approaches (except that many real-time projects are critical, and for that reason the approach is used in real-time systems more than in the other domains); and, in fact, innovative problems might tend to use fault tolerance less than the norm since the nature of the problem is sufficiently complex, and the solutions sufficiently exploratory in nature, that the added complexity of fault tolerance would tend to obscure more important goals. In fact, because fault-tolerant approaches are more complex than their alternatives, many suggest that fault tolerance should *not* be used unless it is absolutely necessary.

8.2.6 AUTOMATIC DESIGN CHECKING

Most design representation approaches now are accompanied by automatic checking CASE tools which ensure that the designer, in creating the design representation, has followed the necessary rules. Those rules may simply be about the requirements of the representation technique, such as the need for dataflow diagram boxes to be connected in some organized way to the whole, or they may be about the design itself, such as the need for all data items to be both defined and referenced in a program design language representation.

These automatic design-checking tools tend to be quite methodology-specific, and it is difficult to say more about them. There is little to be said about them from a project type viewpoint. Using automated design checking is always better than not using it. Except for critical applications, where all the stops should be pulled out in error removal, and thus automated design checking is super-essential, this technique is necessary for all project types, no matter their size, domain, or innovativeness (but not, of course, sufficient. Most automated error checkers tend to be more about syntax than semantics; a design that passes an automated checker is not necessarily a correct design for the problem at hand).

8.2.7 DESIGN REVIEW

Design reviews are the process of using problem- and software-knowledgeable inspectors to examine a proposed design to see if it is necessary and sufficient to solve the problem at hand. Reviews come in many different levels of formality, are recommended in many different forms (from group reviews to individual inspections), and come at different points in the design process (preliminary design reviews check to see if the designers are going in the right direction; critical design reviews check to see if the designers got to the right destination).

There is now considerable data to show that design reviews are one of the most effective error-removal processes, and are cost-effective as well. The form and formality of the review is less important than the rigor of the review. (In a previous section we noted that formality is about following rules, while rigor is about concentration and skill). That is, if the reviewers are conscientiously concentrating on the issue of whether the design is correct for the problem at hand, then it does not much matter whether or not formal rules are followed in the review process. (It should be noted that this is a controversial statement; advocates of design review formality would probably differ with it. However, a recent empirical study [Rifkin 1995] tends to support this viewpoint.)

Because of their general usefulness, design reviews should be used on all types of projects. For critical or large or innovative projects, they should be intense and thorough; for small and noncritical projects, they may be informal. (The less critical the project, in general, the less formal the review need be.) The issue of application domain is not terribly relevant here.

Reference

[Rifkin 1995] Stan Rifkin and Lionel Deimel, "Applying Program Comprehension Techniques to Improve Software Inspections," *The Software Practitioner*, May 1995.

8.2.8 TOP-DOWN AND BOTTOM-UP IMPLEMENTATION

Here we switch from the design phase to the implementation phase. And, unfortunately, a couple of familiar terms are given two new and unfamiliar definitions.

Top-down implementation is the process of building a software product in whole increments. That is, each new and evolving version of the product is a whole product, designed to be tested via an evolving integration test.

Bottom-up implementation is the process of building a software product in small and separate components, testing them thoroughly individually before they are integrated together as a whole.

Note that these two meanings are somewhat related, but still quite different, from the definitions of top-down and bottom-up design.

As with top-down, bottom-up, and hard-part-first design, these two implementation approaches are probably best when used together. That is, the goals of the top-down approach (having a verified version of the integrated product at each step of the construction process) and of the bottom-up approach (having well tested components before they are attached to an integrated whole) should both be achieved in most projects.

To do this, key components should be subjected to the bottom-up approach, well tested as units before being attached to the whole. But at the same time, the build-and-test process of the total project should be conducted in integrated fashion. Tested key components should be attached to the integrated whole as they become available.

Note that reuse is essentially a bottom-up approach in both the design and implementation senses. That is, reusable components are created separately and tested individually before being used in a project.

The traditional approach to building software has been bottom-up, with unit testing preceding integration testing preceding system testing. But the top-down approach has sufficient advantages—giving early visibility of project progress to both managers and customers/users—that recently it has been commonly used as well.

Regarding project types, probably neither approach is better than the other for any particular kind of project. Perhaps for critical software it is important to emphasize thorough bottom-up testing as well as thorough top-down testing. But otherwise, for all types of projects—large or small, all application domains, critical or not, innovative or not—a combination of top-down and bottom-up implementation is the best way to proceed.

8.2.9 MODULAR DESIGN AND IMPLEMENTATION

Probably the single most important technique for building quality software is the use of modular design and implementation. By means of modules, functions are isolated into separate components, making them easier to design, build, comprehend, test, and modify. Good modularity is the best way to achieve the principles of abstraction and single-point control on a software project.

The benefits of modular programming are extolled in many places, and are so well-known in both theory and practice that they need not be repeated here. It is sufficient to say that modularity should be used on all types of software projects, regardless of size, domain, criticality, or innovativeness.

It is interesting to note that the "object" of object-oriented programming is an expanded type of module, where the object consists of one or more data items and the operations to be performed on them. This new form of module, sometimes called a "package" (in Ada, for example), is more data- than function-focused, but the benefits are still the same.

8.2.10 STRUCTURED CODING

Structured coding is that part of the structured methodologies having to do with rules for writing code. In this book, we do not deal with the structured methodologies as a whole, but rather as disaggregated components. (For example, we dealt not with structured design but with top-down design. The meaning of "structured" has tended to be diluted as more and more vendors have used it to apply to whatever they were currently advocating. In addition, the structured methodologies tend to package various techniques in such a way that we lose sight of the significance of the trees in order to appreciate the structured forest.)

Structured coding is coding using the forms sequence, if-then-else, do-while and do-until, and case. Note that the goto form is intentionally omitted from the list of forms.

Structured coding is better than nonstructured coding. But the important question is "How much better?" The unfortunate answer is that we do not know. There have been no significant studies measuring the benefits of structured coding versus its opposite (commonly called, derisively, "spaghetti code").

Fortunately, there is little cost to writing structured code as opposed to spaghetti code, so there is no excuse for not doing so. (Some programming languages, however, are better for writing structured code than others. Fortunately, as languages are upgraded, those languages that were poor at structured code have had the necessary forms included, so that—except for 4GLs, where structure can be a problem—language is now rarely a barrier.)

Like modularity, structured coding is good and worth doing regardless of project type. If the appropriate language support is available, structured code should be used on all projects, regardless of size, domain, criticality, or innovativeness.

8.2.11 HIGH-ORDER LANGUAGE

The spectrum of languages tends to run between two extremes: languages close to the computer (such as assembly language) and languages close to the problem being solved (such as 4GLs). In between are the vast majority of languages, which are somewhat close to the machine and somewhat close to the problem. For example, C tends to be on the machine side of the spectrum, and COBOL tends to be on the problem side (for business applications, the domain for which it was defined). Pascal and Modula are somewhat closer to the center, although they tend to be focused on systems and scientific problems. Most languages, in fact, are intended for a certain class of problems; no matter how hard the recent advocates of Ada try to make it into an all-purpose language, it is important to remember that its original requirements lay in the real-time and systems domains, and there was never any intent during its design to make it useful for anything else.

There are several key parameters in choosing a programming language for a problem to be solved:

- The highest-level language that solves the problem at hand should be used.

- The language most compatible with the application domain at hand should be used.

- The language with the most effective compiler should be used.

These parameters are stated in the order of their importance. That is, software problem-solvers should always take the going in position that the language chosen will be the highest level available. (High-level languages are easier to write, easier to read, easier to test, and easier to maintain.)

But note that the language chosen must "solve the problem at hand." Many problem-focused 4GLs have inadequacies that limit their applicability, and often they simply fail to address the complex problems we tend to encounter today. Generally, the compromise of choice is to use a full-functioned 3GL (although in certain rare cases, primarily those where efficiency or machine dependency is critical, assembler must be used instead).

The issue then tends to be "which 3GL"? And here, the second parameter kicks in. Some languages are much better at solving certain classes of problems than others. COBOL, for example, for all the fun made of it, has many ready-made features to address business applications that would have to be designed and programmed if another language were used. Similarly, C and Modula and Pascal are super languages for the systems programming domain, and COBOL is abysmal at handling this class of problem.

Generally, the choice of languages can stop after the second parameter. But sometimes, especially on a hardware platform where there is limited compiler support, the availability and quality of the compiler come into play. This first becomes an issue if, for example, there is a requirement for efficiency, and the only language processors are interpreters rather than compilers. Since interpreters often run 100 times slower than compiled code, clearly they are a poor choice for projects that will consume large amounts of computer time. The same kinds of choices, at a much lower significance level, occur in the efficiency of generated code. It is easy to build a compiler that generates mediocre code; it is difficult to build one that generates optimal code. Again, if efficiency matters, the 2-1 or 3-1 inefficiency of a poor optimizing compiler may swing the choice of language to one that supports good code generation. (Benchmark applications must be run to determine code efficiency). And, of course, if a compiler frequently generates erroneous code (which seldom happens any more), the programmer should switch to another compiler (or language, if necessary).

We have already seen that the choice of language is primarily application-dependent. Business applications, for example, should use 4GLs whenever they solve the problem at hand and COBOL otherwise. (C or C++ is also an appropriate choice in some business applications, especially on new client/server applications, where the complexity lies in getting machines to talk to each other more than in solving a business problem.) For scientific applications, Fortran, Pascal, and Modula are appropriate choices. For systems applications, C (or perhaps C++) is the best choice. The same is true for real-time applications, except that Ada should be added to the list. Notice that there are few 4GLs currently available for the scientific, systems, or real-time domains. Notice also that we have not mentioned the object-oriented languages, except for C++. Object Orientation brings up some sticky issues in this area. We believe that the choice of language should be application-dependent rather than methodology-dependent. Since there have been few studies of the applicability of Smalltalk and Eiffel (for example) to different domains, it is difficult to decide what applications they are good for.

With respect to the other project types and the choice of language, size, criticality, and innovativeness should play a considerably smaller role.

8.2.12 CODING STANDARDS AND ENFORCERS

The issue of coding standards was dealt with earlier. Two important points were made there: that coding standards are important but can be overdone, and that coding standards, once defined, must be enforced.

What kinds of coding standards are we talking about here? Things like naming conventions for variables, language form limitations (minimizing GOTOs, for example), commentary conventions, interface structures, and so on. There are lots of books with lots of lists of appropriate coding standards, including the corresponding section of *Building Quality Software*.

Once we have avoided the problems of profuse standards and unenforced standards, the rest is relatively easy. Standards should be chosen by knowledgeable professionals and subject to consensus approval, and enforcement mechanisms (and escape mechanisms, for those rare occasions where standards inhibit problem-solving) should be designed and implemented. Enforcement should be performed by "auditor" CASE tools in an automated fashion whenever possible; but unfortunately, many standards can only be checked by a human being. For example, a standard restricting the use of the GOTO statement can usually be checked with an automated tool, but a standard requiring that variable names be meaningful cannot. Note that the ability to check with automated tools should not drive the choice of standards; some of the most important standards (those related to creating modular designs and code, for example) cannot be checked automatically.

Does project type enter into the matter? To some extent, the answer is yes. For example, large projects are more likely to need comprehensive coding standards than small ones (and the cost of creating enforcement techniques is pro-rated over a larger amount of code). Different standards may be appropriate to different application domains. (For example, since COBOL is a business-domain-language, COBOL-specific standards tend to be application-oriented.) The role of standards is probably not terribly relevant in critical projects (remember that too many standards is just as bad as too few. Critical projects do *not* need more standards than other projects). And on innovative projects standards may play a less vital role, especially since innovation sometimes demands release from standards in order to make problem solution possible.

8.2.13 STANDARDIZED ELEMENTS

This level of standardization goes beyond coding standards. For example, an enterprise may elect to standardize on an operating system, or a programming language (chosen relevant to application domain, we hope!), or a set of CASE tools, or a hardware type (such as IBM or Intel), or even a library of reusable modules. These kinds of standards are generally useful for the same reason that standards in general are useful: they make things more predictable.

The issues of this kind of standardization are, however, quite complex. The roles of project type—size, domain, criticality, and innovativeness—are intertwined here in complex ways. For example, an innovative problem may demand escape from some established standards. A large project may have enough weight to create its own standards, or may be so important as to require its using established standards! A critical project, similarly, may need to escape from certain standards to achieve high reliability, or it may need to conform to certain others for the same reason!

Thus, it is possible to say that standardizing elements is often a wise approach, but it is difficult to say much more than that.

8.2.14 WIZARDS

No matter how much technical wisdom is poured into improving our ways of building quality software, there is still some wisdom that is simply unattainable except through key people. Such people have come to be called, in computing circles, "wizards." A computing organization needs one or more wizards to bail software people out of problems that they seem otherwise unable to escape.

Wizards may be experts in certain languages/compilers, or operating systems, or application domains, or hardware boxes, or any of a number of other areas where specialties develop in the software field. And, with respect to project types, the need is almost universal—the wizard is needed, at one time or another, on most projects.

A well-chosen wizard is worth more than all the technologies and tools and process improvements that an enterprise might muster. The literature on individual differences, reporting on how much better (or worse) some software people are than others, consistently finds that some software people are up to 30 times better than others. Considering that the pay range for software developers ranges over roughly only a factor of 2, or at most 3, those 30 times-better people are the biggest bargain in the software business! Not all of those top software people are wizards, of course—some of them work away quietly in a corner, and only their peers may know who they really are. But in general, wizards are drawn from that pool of top people, and their wizardry is intimately correlated with their 30-1 rating.

Types of projects which may particularly need access to wizards are those that are complex (and large projects are frequently complex simply because of their size); those that are critical (important problems must be confronted and solved, never allowed to linger); and those that are innovative ("How do I accomplish X?" [where X is difficult] is a question that frequently arises on innovative projects).

8.2.15 DESIGN AND IMPLEMENTATION SUMMARY

Let us review techniques and tools for improving software design and implementation.

First, we presented the 9000-3 requirements for design and implementation. They emphasized a disciplined process, paying attention to input-output and interfaces, use of a systematic methodology and a useful collection of methods/tools, using lessons learned, producing testable and maintainable products, an emphasis on standards, and the use of reviews.

But that was it. Probably more than any other life-cycle phase of software, the 9000-3 requirements are barely adequate, certainly not sufficient.

Even the initial 9000-3 requirement to carry out design in a disciplined matter must be interpreted. The most important part of design is cognitive and creative, and discipline is not necessarily the best way to achieve good, successful design. Still, we have seen that—in the spirit of 9000-3—discipline is meant to imply that the design is to be correct, and with that interpretation it is difficult to find fault.

The admonition of 9000-3 to pay attention to input-output and interfaces is correct, of course, but also insufficient. Good design is about much more than I/O and interfaces, and the designer who literally follows 9000-3 on this subject will be in deep trouble, producing a design that omits such key factors as algorithms, databases and structures, performance issues, and many more. With that in mind, we presented several approaches to design that are much more encompassing than 9000-3.

The requirements to use design methodologies and implementation methods and tools also need interpretation. The key issue is not whether to use a methodology, but which one to use. And the choice is sufficiently complex that more advice and/or direction is needed. The portions of this section on process/data/object/event and the top-down/bottom-up/hard-part-first approaches are intended to address this issue more fully.

The suggestion to make use of lessons learned is excellent advice. Software projects in the past have made far too little use of lessons learned. We strongly suggest the use of the "experience factory" concept originated by the NASA-Goddard Software Engineering Laboratory (which includes representation from the University of Maryland Computer Science department and Computer Sciences Corp.) for documentation, retention, and accessing lessons learned. But note that this issue goes well beyond design and implementation in its importance—lessons learned should be retained and built on for all phases of the software life cycle.

9000-3 also requires that the design should facilitate testing, maintenance, and use. Once again, this is excellent advice, but knowing how to achieve it is as important as the commitment to do it. The sections on testing and maintenance, to follow, include concepts needed to flesh out this advice.

9000-3 is also wise to require both design and implementation reviews. There are, however, certain circumstances in which the requirement can and should be eased, using informal rather than formal review processes. Those circumstances have been discussed in this section.

Once again, we see that 9000-3 is emphasizing *what* ought to be done but not *how* to achieve it. What we have tried to do in this section is suggest ways to achieve not just what is required by ISO 9000-3, but rather the achievement of a successful software product as well. In Table 8.2, we see quite a mix of approaches to achieving successful design and implementation. Some are application-domain-dependent (methodologies, for example); some are appropriate to all types of projects (e.g., modular and structured design and implementation), and some are subject to varying degrees of formality depending on project characteristics (e.g., reviews).

As with preceding summary sections of this chapter, it is important to acknowledge that the material in this section (and the following table) is subject to legitimate disagreement. That is, not everyone would agree with the relationships drawn here between techniques/tools and project type. This material constitutes our recommendations on the matter of techniques and tools for successful design and implementation; the recommendations of others might be different.

Table 8.2 Project Types vs. Techniques: Design and Implementation

Technique/Tool	Project Type:									
	Size		Application				Criticality		Innova-tiveness	
	Lg	Sm	Bus	Sci	Sys	R-T	High	Low	High	Low
Process, data, object, event	->	->	D	P	O	E	<-	<-	O?	O?
Top-down, bottom-up, hard-part-first	All	All	All	All	All	All	All	All	All	All
Representation Should be based on methodology (above)										
Fault tolerance Should be based on criticality alone										
Automatic checking	Use if available for all projects									
Design review	YT	I	Y	Y	Y	Y	YT	Y?	YT	Y

Technique/Tool	Project Type:									
	Size		Application				Criticality		Innova-tiveness	
	Lg	Sm	Bus	Sci	Sys	R-T	High	Low	High	Low
Top-down, bottom-up implementation	All	All	All	All	All	All	All	All	All	All
Modular design and implementation	Y	Y	Y	Y	Y	Y	Y	Y	Y	Y
Structured coding	Y	Y	Y	Y	Y	Y	Y	Y	Y	Y
High-order language	Use the highest that solves the problem, the choice based on application domain									
Coding standards and enforcers	YT	Y	Y	Y	Y	Y	YT	Y	Y?	Y
Standardized elements	Use when available for problem at hand									
Wizards	Y	Y?	Y?	Y	Y	Y	Y	Y?	Y	Y?

Legend:

All = Use a mix of the listed techniques

D = Data-oriented

E = Event-oriented

I = Informally

O = Object-oriented

O? = Object if appropriate

P = Process-oriented

N = No

Y = Yes

YT = Yes, thoroughly

Y? = Yes, but not vital

-> = Depends on application domain

<- = Depends on application domain

8.3 TESTING AND VALIDATION

The test and validation portions of 9000-3 are focused primarily on test documentation rather than the test process itself. It concentrates heavily on test planning, and barely gestures at how to perform testing activities. The section on validation is only one paragraph long. Basically, here is what 9000-3 requires:

- There may be several levels of testing, from item to product, and several different approaches to testing.

- The test plan should contain test cases, test data, and expected results.

- The test plan should describe the types of tests to be conducted (e.g., functional tests, performance tests).

- The test plan should describe the test environment, including test tools.

- Test readiness evaluation should examine user documentation, personnel requirements, and the criteria for determining completion of testing.

Regarding the conduct of testing, 9000-3 requires:

- Test results should be recorded as defined in the relevant specification.

- Any problems encountered during testing should be noted, and those responsible for repairing them notified, with repair work tracked.

- Areas changed should be identified and retested.

- Test adequacy and relevancy should be evaluated.

- The hardware and software configuration should be "considered" (!) and documented.

With respect to validation, 9000-3 is even less explicit:

- The complete product should be validated under user-like conditions.

Once again, these levels of requirement are necessary but not sufficient for defining a good quality system. The remainder of this section will deal with specific techniques that may be used to improve the value of testing and validation. But first, let us discuss those issues in the testing and validation subject area that cause significant controversy in the field.

8.3.1 TESTING AND VALIDATION ISSUES

There are some major differences of opinion in the field about ways of accomplishing testing and validation. Those differences are discussed in the material that follows.

8.3.1.1 Testing and Inspection

Testing is the process of executing an evolving software product in order to see if the results it produces are the ones it is expected to produce. Testing, therefore, is a dynamic process.

Inspection is the process of examining an evolving software product to see if any flaws can be detected statically (without executing it).

The major issue here is "which is more effective, testing or inspection?" Interestingly, for this issue the answer is crisp and clear: Inspection is both more effective (in terms of the number of errors it finds) and cost-effective (in terms of the cost of finding those errors). That is an interesting resolution of the issue because, unlike most issues where the answer is not clearcut (otherwise, it wouldn't remain an issue!), there is no doubt about this answer. Study after study in place after place has found that inspection finds more errors, more cheaply, than testing.

Why, then, does testing vs. inspection remain an issue? There are two reasons:

1. **Tradition**. Testing has been the chief means of error removal since the beginnings of the field (in the 1950s). The value of inspections has been known since sometime in the 1970s, and the research findings that demonstrated its superiority tended to be products of the 1980s, but even today testing is the prime means of software error removal, and often inspection is not performed at all. Inspection is a laborious, complex, challenging, and demanding way of finding errors. At the time inspection is being performed, it feels like a much more expensive and much less effective alternative to testing. It is taking a long time to overcome that mindset.

2. **Conflict**. Once it began to be seen that inspection was superior to testing, a few fringe people in the field began to suggest it as a replacement for testing. It is important to note here that replacing testing with *anything* else is one of the biggest mistakes that can be made in the software field. The reason is that no matter how effective inspection is in finding errors, inspection is based on the mindset that the design and requirements are basically correct, and the purpose of inspection is to find errors through finding not only things that won't work correctly, but things that are not consistent with the design and requirements specs. That is a necessary condition for error removal, but not a sufficient one. Testing the software product allows those perusing the results to realize not only that there are errors, but that the software requirements, as stated, are not what is or was desired. Thus, any attempt to minimize or eliminate testing— whether by inspections, formal verification (see below), or assuming that fault-tolerant software will detect and overcome its own errors (and each of those has been used by some to draw the conclusion that testing can be elimi-

nated!)—is a major mistake. Or, to put that another way, *the process of software error removal must be a blend of techniques used to complement one another.*

8.3.1.2 Formal Verification

Formal verification, also known as proof of correctness, is no doubt the most controversial topic in the software field. Formal verification is the static process of inspecting a software product using certain mathematical-proof-like approaches in order to find inconsistencies between the product and its specification. It is discussed in more detail later. The opinions on formal verification range from completely negative to completely positive! For example, most practitioners have no interest in the process because it is difficult to comprehend, difficult and error-prone to conduct, and is dependent on the specification being correct in order to be effective. Those academics who believe in formal verification, on the other hand, believe in it so strongly that:

1. They have made it a part of the standard computer science curriculum, starting with beginning-level courses.

2. They have tried to institutionalize it, making it a required form of error removal by law (in England, the Ministry of Defense requires it for embedded real-time software applications).

As can be seen, the differences of opinion here are radically different, from "it's worthless" to "you *must* do it." And those poles-apart positions have both been present in the field since shortly after the advent of the concept in the late 1960s. You would expect, of course, that such a longstanding and dramatic difference would have been settled long ago with some sort of experiments conducted to evaluate the relative merits of formal verification and its alternatives. Amazingly, that has never been done! Instead, the controversy rages on with all the fervor of a religious war, erupting periodically when a paper is published taking a strong stand on one end of the polar separation, and the advocates at the other end try to tear it to shreds and make personal attacks on its authors!

The reader of this book is invited to form his or her own opinion of the merits of the matter. However, in this book the authors side with the practitioners. We choose not to recommend it for any project types, even for critical applications, unless the tester/validator has used all other error removal processes and is willing to spend more time and more money for further confidence in the product's reliability. There are cheaper and better ways, we believe, to remove errors.

8.3.1.3 Cleanroom Approaches

A methodology is the packaging of a collection of individual techniques into a cohesive whole. The purpose of creating a methodology is to create effective, holistic ways of accomplishing what is desired. Methodologies originated in the software field in the 1970s with the advent of structured approaches, and competing methodologies have been created ever since.

Cleanroom is a methodology for error removal. As such, it packages together these ideas:

1. Formal verification is used by the developers to find errors.

2. Testing is never performed by the developers, only by independent test groups, and only after formal verification has been performed and the errors so found removed.

3. Testing is entirely statistical.

In other words, Cleanroom is a testing methodology that packages together formal verification, purely independent testing, and statistical testing.

It is difficult to examine a methodology as a whole, since invariably it consists of diverse and separable techniques. In this book, in order to examine methodologies, we disaggregate them—break them into their constituent technologies—and then examine those separately. You may have noted, for example, that the structured methodologies are never discussed as such in this book, but that many of the constituent elements—top-down design, structured coding, and so forth—*are* discussed.

What makes Cleanroom particularly interesting and worth mentioning as a whole is that (a) it has powerful and well-known advocates, and (b) real experiments have been conducted into its value, experiments that have shown largely positive results. Let us, then, begin the disaggregation and examination of Cleanroom.

The first element of Cleanroom is formal verification. The alert reader will see a head-on collision coming here! We have already taken the position, in this book, that formal verification has minimal value. Obviously, then, we find Cleanroom to be a flawed methodology right off the bat!

Interestingly, in most of the experiments conducted to evaluate Cleanroom, the researchers have elected to substitute something they called "rigorous inspection" for formal verification. And the positive findings have been made with this substitution in effect. (The substitution was rationalized by the fact that formal verification is too hard to learn; and, of course, the fact that the results were positive without it tends to support the decision made!) Rigorous inspection has been dealt with earlier in this book; based on the findings discussed there, and the Cleanroom experimental findings, it is once again apparent that rigorous inspections are a superior method of error removal, and an effective substitute for formal verification.

The second element of Cleanroom is independent testing, using a group different from the developers to create and run the test cases. Independent testing is further discussed later in this book. It is sufficient to say here that independent testing is an effective form of error removal because it is staffed with people whose goal is to find errors (whereas developers, even those very objective in their error searching, have the goal of eventually *not* finding errors). Note that Cleanroom goes further than independent testing; it requires that developers *never* do testing, instead doing formal verification (or rigorous inspection!) before turning the product over for independent testing. That in itself is a controversial issue. Most software professionals feel that it is important for the developers to be part of the testing process. They are more likely than independent testers, for example, to know where the difficult and therefore error-prone parts of the software are, and concentrate the testing on those areas.

One of the most interesting experimental findings about Cleanroom is that its use removes over 90% of software errors before testing even begins. But this finding, considered in depth, actually suggests that the major contribution of Cleanroom is what happens *before* testing begins. Thus, independent testing, for all its intuitive wisdom, cannot be considered to be the most important element of Cleanroom. (Once again, we see that rigorous inspections, substituted for formal verification, are the most important element!)

The third element of Cleanroom is statistical testing. This topic also will be discussed in more detail later in this book. But briefly, statistical testing is the act of:

1. Creating and executing test cases randomly

2. Tailoring this randomization to the software product's "operational profile;" that is, taking steps to ensure that the randomly chosen test cases reflect typical intended product usage

3. Drawing statistical conclusions about the effectiveness of the test cases, saying things like "97% of the test cases are currently running successfully"

The principal difference between statistical and traditional testing techniques is that traditional testing selects test cases for a particular reason (such as to explore the functioning of a complex portion of a program, or to test known exception conditions), and statistical testing does not. The effect is somewhat like firing a gun: traditional testing is about firing rifle shots at chosen targets; statistical testing is about firing shotgun blasts (where the blasts are concentrated on areas of expected heavy usage).

We have already seen that the most important benefits of Cleanroom are achieved before testing begins. It is thus apparent that the experiments demonstrating the value of Cleanroom do not allow us to draw any conclusions about the benefits of statistical testing. Other studies have shown that statistical testing is more effective in lowering software mean time between failure. (Some say that is not a surprising finding, since mean time between failure is a conclusion drawn from random results, and statistical testing is based on random tests.) However, there are serious problems with statistical testing:

1. In traditional testing, there is the expectation of a predetermined test oracle, a set of known correct answers for the problem at hand. With statistical testing, since the test cases are random, there is no convenient way of determining a test oracle. (Note that ISO 9000-3 requires "expected results" for test cases; if statistical testing is used, care must be taken to keep its use in conformance.)

2. Traditional testing theory suggests that testing should be concentrated in certain areas (one author speaks of "biased" faults, those which programmers tend to make commonly; another speaks of "error guessing," a (legitimate) testing technique in which the tester uses their knowledge of the product to aim test cases at vulnerable places). Statistical testing cannot support test case concentration effectively.

3. Perhaps the most common, and at the same time damaging, software errors are those that occur on exception conditions, portions of the software not in its mainstream but in its handling of unexpected conditions. (For example, a recent major failure in the telephone system was aggravated by an error in the exception handling of the system's software; an original error which might have been isolated and corrected was instead propagated by the exception handler, taking the entire system down for a matter of hours.) Statistical testing that focuses on operational profiles may well be ineffective in removing exception errors.

However, there is one final important point to be made in favor of statistical testing. It is the only form of testing that produces a conclusion meaningful to the customer/user. Whereas traditional testing allows us to make claims of the form "85% of the software's logic has been tested," Cleanroom allows us to say "97% of operational profile test cases are running successfully." As a software developer, I am probably at least as interested in statements about coverage as in statements about success; but the customer or user gets very little out of coverage knowledge. Recall the position, taken early in this section, that error removal must be a blend of techniques. It is our belief, in this book, that traditional testing should not be *replaced* by statistical testing, but that statistical testing can be used to complement traditional approaches.

Looking at Cleanroom from something of a distance, although its notions of formal verification and removing the developer from the testing process appear to be dubious, the notions of rigorous inspection by the developer, independent testing, and statistical testing all have at least some merit.

References

[Mills 1987] Harlan D. Mills, Mike Dyer, and Richard Liger, "Cleanroom
   Software Engineering," *IEEE Software*, Sept. 1987.
[Shelby 1987] Richard W. Selby, Victor R. Basili, and F. Terry Baker,
   "Cleanroom Software Development: An Empirical Evaluation," *IEEE
   Transactions on Software Engineering*, Sept. 1987.

8.3.2 STATIC METHODS

So much for the issues of the testing and validation
phase. Let us move on to testing and validation techniques.
We will divide these techniques into static and dynamic
approaches.

Static methods of testing and validation are those that
do not require the software to execute during the error
removal process. Four forms of static error removal are discussed here: desk checking, peer code review, structural
analysis, and proof of correctness (formal verification).

8.3.2.1 Desk Checking

Desk checking is whatever the software developer can
do at his or her desk to seek and remove errors without
causing the software to execute. Typically, it takes these
forms:

- Reviewing the program source code for faults

- Doing whatever is needed to create test oracles and to
  verify test case outputs

- "Playing computer"—mentally simulating program execution in order to understand and verify program logic
  and data flow

As the software field has progressed to computers on the
desk, not tucked away in locked and/or glass-walled rooms,
the use of desk checking has diminished. It is often easier to

launch program execution at a desktop computer in order to run real test cases and analyze their results than it is to do computer-less desk checking. For the most part, this is an improvement. But desk checking often involves a more in-depth form of involvement with, and understanding of, the as-built code than does relying on the computer to generate good or bad results. As a result, desk checking will probably always be at least a supplemental form of error removal. It is appropriate to all types of software projects, regardless of size, domain, criticality, or innovativeness, although—like all error removal techniques—it is especially important to critical projects.

8.3.2.2 Peer Code Review

Peer code review is a process by which a team of software people do an in-depth review of a software product or part of a product. It is also known by other terms, such as code inspection, code verification, or code walkthrough.

By whatever name, peer code review must involve:

- Two or more people (if only one, the developer, is involved, it is "desk checking")

- Rigorous reading of the code (it is the required rigor that makes reviews as taxing as they are)

- Looking for faults as well as standards nonconformance

There is some flexibility in the method of conducting the peer code review. Reviews may be meetings, or they may be performed by separate individuals at locations of their choosing. (There is mixed evidence of the effectiveness of these two approaches; although one would expect some synergism from a meeting, one might also expect more rigor if the reviewer is allowed to concentrate in isolation. Experimental studies support both of these points of view!) Several studies have shown that there is an optimal number of reviewers, but those studies differ on what that number is! (The range from two to four appears to be optimal, however, and that covers all study findings.) There are differences of opinion on the required formality of reviews. The most formal require having rules for the meetings, training for participants, and specific roles played by attendees. Others take the position that it is the rigor of the process, not its formality, that matters most.

It is important to remember that reviews are for identifying problems, not solving them. A review must not allow itself to get bogged down in finding solutions. Rigorous reviews are taxing and time-consuming, and any technique that keeps them focused yet optimally short is a good technique.

We have already seen a discussion of the fact that such reviews or inspections are the most effective and cost-effective error removal processes. Because of that, they are appropriate for all types of projects. The greatest need for complete reviews/inspections is on projects that are critical; the least is on small projects. Because of the cost and complexity of reviews, a compromise position is sometimes taken wherein only critical parts of the software project are reviewed. For very large projects, where the cost of reviewing every line of every component might be staggering, this may be an appropriate compromise (assuming that the project is not critical). It may also be an appropriate compromise for the very small project, where the incremental cost of a complete review might cause an otherwise worthwhile project to be infeasible.

8.3.2.3 Structural Analysis

This form of static checking usually involves some use of the computer, but not to execute the software product itself. Software tools that analyze a program looking for structural flaws are applied to the project's source code to identify specific types of errors.

This is a catch-all term. There are many different forms of structural analysis, and often the tools available to do the work are computer hardware- and/or operating-system-specific. For example, structural analyzers exist to detect:

- Data variables undeclared

- Data variables used before their initialization, or never used

- Use of unauthorized language forms (e.g., GOTO)

- Violations of naming conventions

- Overly complicated constructs (e.g., loops too deeply nested)

- Procedure argument mismatch (between caller and callee)

- Inconsistent procedure call trees (e.g., inadvertent recursion)

- Inconsistent global data (e.g., mismatched *common* blocks)

- Unreachable or missing or erroneous logic

One common form of structural analyzer is the code auditor, which detects violations of coding standards.

The cost of performing structural analysis when an appropriate tool is available is relatively low. As a result, such tools should be used on all project types, regardless of size, domain, criticality, or innovativeness. That is usually true whether the tool is already available in the enterprise, or available as a package to be purchased from a vendor. (Most such tools are priced at under $1000 and are thus cost-effective. Tools that cost more must be evaluated on a case basis.) The problem arises when such tools are *not* available. In that case, careful consideration must be made about the cost and benefit of building such a tool or tools in-house, or contracting for their creation by a tools vendor. For critical projects, if the tool is sufficiently effective it should be built. Similarly, for large projects, effective tools are worth building because the cost can be spread over a much larger budget base. For other types of projects, it is usually undesirable to build such tools specifically for one project.

8.3.2.4 Proof of Correctness (Formal Verification)

We have already seen that this topic is probably the most controversial in the software field. But what is proof of correctness all about?

Proof of correctness is the process of applying mathematical theorem-proving concepts to an evolving software product to determine whether it is consistent with its specification. This is done by breaking the software product into segments, defining input and output assertions for each segment (an input assertion is a statement of what characteristics the input to the segment must have; an output assertion is a similar statement about the output it produces), and demonstrating that, when the program functions, correct output assertions imply correct input assertions. The process is usually manual but may be supplemented by various theorem-prover tools.

It is important to note that proof of correctness is about consistency with the specification rather than correctness; that is, a successful proof demonstrates that the program matches its specification. The use of proof of correctness, therefore, tends to emphasize the use of formal specification languages in order to make the consistency check more viable. Note also that if the specification is incorrect, a program that has been proven to be "correct" will, in fact, not be correct in the broader sense.

Proof of correctness is controversial because, although it is a rigorous and thorough process when it is done correctly, it is also hard to learn and easy to do badly. One software researcher found that most published software "proofs" were themselves flawed. Obviously, an erroneous proof says absolutely nothing about the reliability of the software product to which it has been applied.

As noted previously, we do not recommend the use of proof of correctness techniques. However, we would be flexible about that position under two circumstances:

- The software in question is being built for the British Ministry of Defense, and they will not accept such software unless it is formally verified.

- The project in question is critical, no expense is being spared in finding and removing errors, and all other error removal approaches have also been used.

8.3.3 DYNAMIC METHODS

Dynamic methods of testing and validation are those that require executing the software product using test data. Several such approaches are discussed in what follows.

8.3.3.1 Source Language Debug

Source language debug is the use of a test tool that allows the tester to interact with test results in a high-level testing language. It contrasts with an older form of debug in which the tester had to read machine language dumps. Source language debug makes it convenient to:

- Specify test outputs to be produced

- List variables or logic points to be traced by name

- Produce readable test outputs, with variables identified by name and printed in appropriate format

- Dynamically control debug outputs to be produced

If the source language debug tool is interactive, as they commonly are in the 1990s, it should also provide for breakpoint and resumption at specified points. And if it is really sophisticated, as some personal computer debug tools are, it should provide for invocation of text editor, recompile and rebuild tools, to allow for modifying program or data portions during the debug session.

For much of the early history of the software field, such tools were known but not commonly available. More recently that has changed and now these tools are commonly available. Because of that, it is now possible to recommend their use on all types of projects, regardless of size, domain, criticality, and innovativeness. In fact, if a software shop is operating without source language debug, it should take steps to correct that situation immediately. Using older forms of debug makes no more sense than programming in machine language. The expense of an appropriate debugger is trivial compared to the cost of functioning without one.

8.3.3.2 Assertion Checker

An assertion checker is a tool that allows for preplanning debugging sessions through the provision of statements asserting what should be true at specific points during the program's execution. For example, an assertion checker should provide for such capabilities as:

- Providing legitimate specific or range values for specified program variables

- Providing relationships between/among variables that should hold true

- Tracing all or specified occurrences of certain variables or assertions

- Recording all violations of specified assertions

- Dynamic control of the application of these assertions

- Keeping a log of assertion violations as the program executes

This use of the word "assertion," it should be noted, is somewhat different from its use in proof of correctness technology. There, the assertion is a statement employed in the proof process. Here, it is a statement whose truth is to be checked by the assertion checker tool. The truth or falsity of the assertion in this case has nothing to do with proving a program to be correct; it only provides clues as to whether a program is dynamically executing correctly.

Assertion technology originated in the 1970s and, for a time, looked like a promising new dynamic testing support capability. Some compilers even provided assertion specification capability, and provided dynamic checking facilities as well. But this technology faded with time, and is now little used. If an assertion checker is available, we recommend its use on all types of projects, especially critical ones. But if such a tool is not available—and that is the normal case today—we do not suggest buying or building one.

8.3.3.3 Intentional Failure

Intentional failure is an odd concept in that it involves deliberately causing a program to fail. There are two entirely different reasons for doing so, "error seeding" and "mutation analysis."

8.3.3.3.1 Error Seeding

One of the key questions of the software test process is "How long should we continue testing?" The answer to that question is dependent on how many errors remain in the software product under test.

In an attempt to provide an answer to that question, some software researchers have borrowed an idea from the world of fisheries. There, the analogous question, "How many fish are there in the lake?" is answered by inserting tagged fish into the lake, catching a collection of fish and determining what percentage of them are tagged, and then extrapolating from that percentage (using the known number of fish inserted into the lake) to calculate how many fish were there to begin with. In fisheries, it is an approximation technique generally considered useful if only because there is no other known way of answering the question!

Will the same technique work for counting software errors? The analogous technique is to deliberately create and log ("tag") certain kinds of errors, and then, when the debuggers find ("catch") a collection of errors, determine what percentage were deliberately created and extrapolate the number that were not.

It is an interesting idea, but one that has not proven popular. There are several reasons for that. For one, deliberately inserting errors into software is often considered a form of madness. It is hard enough to find and remove software errors without intentionally creating more! But, more important, the technique works for fish because one tags the same kind of fish as are known to be in the lake. But what kind of software errors should we intentionally create? Presumably, they should be ones like the ones we are trying to find. But what kinds are those? Pursuing this line of reasoning further, the whole idea rapidly falls apart. As a result, we do not recommend this technique for any software projects, regardless of project type.

8.3.3.3.2 Mutation Testing

Another important question in the testing process is "How effective is our collection of test cases?" If they are likely to catch most software errors, then we can be satisfied with what we have. If not, we must add new test cases.

Mutation testing is a way of answering this question. Once again, we deliberately insert errors into the software, in this case to see if, when we run our collection of test cases, their outputs change. If the outputs do not change, then clearly our collection is insufficient to detect the change we made. (The programs with intentionally inserted errors are called "mutants" in the biological sense of the word.)

Once again, problems arise when we try to decide what kinds of errors to introduce. There are nearly infinite variations of errors one could introduce, ranging from deleting an entire statement to changing the last decimal place of a program constant. It is easy to imagine spending great amounts of time building mutants, and in fact the process of building them is supportable with automated tools.

Mutation testing, like error seeding, is little used in practice. However, unlike error seeding, it continues to have a loyal following in the academic theory world. At this point in its evolution, and in spite of its theoretical support, we do not recommend it for any types of software projects, even critical ones.

8.8.3.4 Performance Analysis

Testing and validation are largely about error removal. Most of the other sections of this portion of the book, therefore, are about techniques for finding and eliminating errors.

However, error removal is not the only task of testing. For some applications, getting the performance of the software correct is almost as important as removing its errors. If the requirements call for the software to execute with a certain degree of efficiency, then it is important to find out whether those requirements have been met.

Performance analysis is the generic term for examining program efficiency. There is a large collection of tools available to support it. Some are very simple and can even be hand-coded into the software product—inserting timing checks at the beginning and end of a program part whose time is to be monitored, for example, summing the difference between the two over a long execution. Other techniques are more complicated, sometimes involving analyzers that run at the hardware or operating-system level and probe what is happening in the computer, and monitor where it is happening and how much time is being consumed. The goals of all such tools is usually to:

- See if timing requirements are being met

- Identify program portions where time is being spent

For what kinds of projects is the use of performance analysis desirable? All those which have efficiency requirements specified. And all those which are consuming unreasonable amounts of computer time, even if there were no performance requirements originally.

This statement of need is independent of project size, criticality, or innovativeness. Regarding application domains, it is usually vital for real-time projects, and is case-dependent for the other domains—business, scientific, and systems.

8.3.3.5 Requirements-Driven Testing

In the next four sections, we discuss a collection of approaches for conducting testing that represent "goal-driven testing." That is, each section focuses on a different *goal* that should be considered in the testing process. Later, in the section on acceptance, we will discuss what we call "phase-driven testing"—a collection of testing approaches that should be considered at different *times* in the software testing process. These approaches are complementary—one needs to consider all of the goals in conjunction with all of the phases.

The four goals are:

- Requirements (testing to see if the software product meets its requirements)

- Structure (testing to see if all portions of the software product's structure are performing correctly)

- Risk (concentrated testing to see if high-risk portions of the program are performing correctly)

- Statistics (testing to give the customer a better view of testing progress)

This section of the foursome is about requirements. We call it requirements-driven testing.

This level of testing is the totally necessary but by no means sufficient minimum amount of testing required for any software product. In it, test cases are constructed to demonstrate that each of the explicit requirements stated in the requirements specification are achieved. Often, the completeness of requirements-driven testing is measured by creating a "test case matrix," one that links test cases to requirements, showing which cases test which requirements.

Thorough requirements-driven testing could, in concept, result in an infinite number of test cases. One might wish to test all possible values of each input variable, for example, and that is clearly impossible. In order to constrain the number of test cases (and their cost), we use the notion of "equivalence classes"—one test case represents a number of other possible ones. For example, if a program runs the same for all values of variable alpha between 0 and 10,000, then we need only choose one value in that range to test. It is useful, in defining equivalence classes, to use the notion of "cause-effect graphing," identifying those statements in the requirements that cause things to happen, and those that are the effects of other causes. Test cases may then be chosen to trigger all the causes and produce all the effects. Another useful technique here is the notion of "boundary-value testing," paying special attention to input variable values for which the program may be particularly sensitive. And if our experience with this type of application tells us that certain things are more likely to fail than others, we employ "error guessing" to construct test cases to see what happens in those circumstances.

Requirements-driven testing is often called "black-box testing" because constructing its test cases does not demand any knowledge of the interior workings of the software product. It is an easy form of testing for independent test groups to perform, for example (typically, only developers are capable of performing testing that requires knowledge of how the product is constructed).

Fortunately, by a judicious use of these techniques, a reasonably finite number of test cases will usually serve to do thorough requirements-driven testing. But, in general, testing all of a software product's requirements by no means tests all of its capabilities. And that brings us to structure-driven testing.

But before we move on, it is important to note that requirements-driven testing should be performed on all project types, regardless of size, domain, criticality, or innovativeness. For critical projects, however, requirements-driven test cases should be more thorough, using more test cases per equivalence class and cause/effect, taking more care to identify all boundary values, and spending more time on error guessing.

8.3.3.6 Structure-Driven Testing

We mentioned above that requirements-driven testing is necessary but not sufficient, and we characterized it as black-box testing because it did not require understanding the program's inner workings.

An important supplement to requirements-driven testing is the subject of this section, structure-driven testing. People performing this type of testing will base the construction of test cases on an understanding of how the program is put together, what its structure is. This type of testing is often characterized as "white-box" or "clear-box" testing because one must be able to look inside the software product to do it.

But first, why is something more than requirements-driven testing necessary? The answer lies in the complexity of the software product.

For even a complicated piece of software, there might be no more than a few hundred explicitly stated requirements. But as one sets out to design a solution to the problem defined by those requirements, an explosion of complexity occurs. To create a design to satisfy a stated set of requirements involves defining *how* that requirement is to be satisfied. And in that "how" lies software's complexity. The explosion of complexity that we mentioned is reflected in the number of design statements needed to implement a requirement. Typically, researchers have found, for every requirement there may be 50 or 100 design statements. Some call this a "requirements explosion," in that the explicit requirements of the original specification must be supplemented by implicit requirements to effect a problem solution.

Given that an explosion has occurred, clearly the final software product will be much more complex than the original requirements. Some way of testing this complex, exploded product must be found. That is where structure-driven testing comes in.

The goal of structure-driven testing is to chop the as-built software into segments whose correctness may be conveniently tested. A given test case can then be run against a set of such segments, and we can determine (a) whether all such segments have been tested, and (b) which segments remain to be tested.

There are a variety of ways in which segments might be determined. For a very object- or data-oriented software product, we might like to measure segments in terms of objects or data structures or data flows. More commonly, however, structured testing is about logic segments. Logic segments might be measured at a fairly high level, such as components or modules, but the technology exists to measure segments at the branch level, and that is the technique most commonly used in structure-driven testing. In the most common form of structure-driven testing, we try to identify which straight-line segments of the program (those that lie between branches) have been executed.

Branches occur differently in different programming languages, of course. But, from a structured coding point of view, branches occur at IF-THEN-ELSE, DO (loop), CASE, and GOTO statements. And segments are collections of code that lie between pairs of such branching statements.

Having said all of this, if we had to perform structured testing manually, somehow recording which segments we thought we had tested and which we had not, the task would be nearly impossible. At that level of visibility, even the knowledgeable software developer finds it hard to predict exactly which program segments a given test case will cause to execute. Fortunately, there are tools to support this kind of determination. They will be covered later in the section called "Test Coverage Analyzer."

With requirements-driven testing, it was vital to test 100% of the requirements. Is the same thing true of structure-driven testing?

The answer, unfortunately, is no. The explosion we mentioned earlier, now extrapolated to the segment level and thus considerably larger than the factor of 50 or 100 explosion we mentioned at design time, makes it simply impossible for all but the most trivial software product to do 100% structure-driven testing. Experience has shown that when software developers think they have done a thorough job of testing, about 55–60% of the program structure has been tested! With the aid of structure-driven testing techniques, it is usually fairly easy to raise that to about 90% of the structure. Beyond that, matters get rapidly more complex. To achieve 100% structural test coverage is generally considered impossible (there are exception conditions and other circumstances that are difficult to create test cases to execute, for example). If software has been structurally tested at the 95% level, that may be considered abnormally thorough. But what about the remaining percentage of structure that has not been tested? Experts advise giving up on testing, and instead using particularly intense inspections of those program segments.

It should be noted that even 100% structure-driven testing, as defined here, would not be sufficient. With this approach, we are only determining which pieces of structure have been executed. There are two situations in which this is insufficient:

- A piece of logic has been omitted (structure-driven testing cannot tell us about things that are not there).

- An error would occur only when a collection of segments is executed in a particular sequence (structure-driven testing does not take order of execution into account).

There is some data about the prevalence of these conditions. A fairly simple study of some not very complex software showed that only about 25% of that software's errors could have been detected by the structure-driven techniques presented here; an additional 35% involved omission of needed logic segments, and another 40% occurred only when certain combinations of segments were executed. That is a particularly discouraging finding, since it essentially shows us that the unachievable 100% structure-driven testing is only 25% as good as we would wish it to be!

This is the time, then, to say something important. Software testing is a sampling process. No matter how thoroughly it is conducted, it cannot guarantee that the software product will be error-free. That reinforces the conclusion we came to earlier, that error removal should involve a combination of techniques, with no technique being excluded from the set.

Given all of that, what about project types? First of all, critical projects should try to come as close to 100% structure-driven testing as possible, supplementing that with intensive inspections—and not quit there, but employ as many other error removal techniques as possible. (Other goal-driven approaches are presented below.) For the remainder, noncritical projects of all sizes, domains, and degrees of innovation, the tester should try to achieve at least 85% segment coverage, and use inspection techniques on the remainder.

What is the state of the practice in this regard? Many software organizations are not even aware of the existence of test coverage analysis tools, and thus have little or no idea how much of their software structure has been tested. Perhaps in this topic area is where the greatest leap forward in software reliability remains to be made. One hundred percent structure-driven testing is, as we have seen, not good enough, but it is easy to imagine that the current state of the practice is more like 55%; and that is definitely far from satisfactory.

8.3.3.7 Risk-Driven Testing

If requirements-driven testing and structure-driven testing are not enough, what is the concerned tester to do? The answer may be risk-driven testing—testing that focuses on the worst things that can go wrong.

Suppose lives or large amounts of money are dependent on your software functioning satisfactorily. It is important, under those circumstances, to define the most likely disasters, the largest risks.

Having identified those disasters, work backward from them, identifying places where software faults could cause those disasters to happen. Once those places have been identified (and for the average piece of complex software there may be a lot of them), concentrate on creating a particularly large number of test cases that exercise those places. Input data that makes those places execute must be identified, test cases containing that data created, and the test cases run and evaluated. Note that this is a special form of structure-driven testing, requiring knowledgeable software developer participation, where the structure chosen is based on the riskiness of failure of that structure.

For what kinds of software projects is risk-driven testing appropriate? Clearly, here the answer is critical projects. Unless the project is critical, there is probably little motivation to use this approach, assuming that proper requirements-driven and structure-driven testing has been done.

8.3.3.8 Statistics-Driven Testing

There is one remaining form of goal-oriented testing, statistics-driven testing. Here, test cases are generated randomly, usually based on a typical operational profile of the software's intended usage. The intent here is to let testing simulate actual product usage. Those who advocate statistics-driven testing tend to suggest its use in place of some of the preceding goal-driven testing approaches, particularly in place of structure-driven testing. Those advocates believe that typical test cases are more useful in error removal than those defined by the software's structure. In addition, although those advocates do not say so, the fact that statistics-driven testing can be done by independent testers, while structure-driven testing cannot, may play a role in their advocacy. Recall that the Cleanroom process, of which statistics-driven testing is one component, is an attempt to divorce software developers from all testing.

The problem with statistics-driven testing, as we have already noted in the Cleanroom section of this book, is that it tends to under-emphasize the testing of exception conditions, and it is difficult to construct test oracles when using it. It seems far more effective and efficient to the authors of this book to focus testing on places where the developers see a need, rather than on the happenstance of random generation.

Still, there is a reason for *supplementing* the previous testing approaches with statistics-driven ones. As we mentioned earlier, being able to say that 100% of the requirements have been tested may give too much confidence to the potential customers and users of the software product, and saying that 85% of the structure has been tested says nothing meaningful at all to the customer or user. If it is desirable or necessary to make statements to the customers/users that measure testedness in terms meaningful to them, statistical testing is an excellent approach. What could be more important to the user than knowing how likely the software is to be able to execute his or her input data satisfactorily?

As a result, we advocate statistics-driven testing only under that condition, independent of project size, application domain, or innovativeness. For those projects that are critical, where the more testing is done the more likely the project is to succeed, statistical testing is yet another supplemental testing technique, and therefore tends to be worthwhile (as long as it does not cause the tester to do less structure-driven or risk-driven testing).

8.3.3.9 Test Coverage Analyzer

In the section of this book on structure-driven testing, we mentioned the fact that a tool was available to measure testedness. The test coverage analyzer is that tool.

The test coverage analyzer answers such questions as

- How much of the structure of the software is tested by the test case set?

- Which portions of the structure have not been tested by the test case set?

It does so by doing these things:

- Prior to execution of the test set, it "instruments" the program to be tested by inserting code to count the number of executions of each portion of the structure.

- During execution of the test set, it counts executions by segment and prepares those counts for cumulative display/printout.

- Following execution of the test set, the counts are displayed/printed, showing cumulative totals by program portion over all test cases.

Program portions are usually logic segments connecting branch points, as discussed in the section on structure-driven testing. However, test coverage analyzer tools have been created which can break programs into other kinds of portions, such as modules or components.

Traditionally, test coverage analyzers have examined logic coverage of programs. However, there is currently research going on to examine dataflows instead, where a program portion is defined to consist of definitions (points where specific variables are assigned values) and edges (connections between definitions and references for those variables). Such a tool might be useful for more data-oriented software, such as business applications. However, there is a problem with test coverage at the dataflow level. The intent of the technique is to track coverage by the data flow of a variable; however, it is not possible to track dataflow for subscripted or pointer variables which have variable subscripts/pointers, and there appears to be no solution to this problem on the horizon. This problem, however, has not prevented researchers from conducting ongoing research into the uses of data flow test coverage. For example, Horgan [1994] discusses an empirical study to relate dataflow coverage and software quality. Because of the intense research interest in this topic area, it would be wise for practitioners to keep abreast of progress here.

Regarding applicability of these techniques to particular project types, then, we would recommend that logic test coverage analyzers be used whenever structure-driven testing is used (there is no other effective way to measure structure coverage). We would only recommend the use of dataflow test coverage analyzers, at present, for those critical applications that are heavily dependent on dataflow, are not much concerned with subscripted and pointer variables, and can afford the extra cost of an emerging technology not in software's mainstream. (We suspect that this would be a very small set!)

Reference

[Horgan 1994] Joseph R. Horgan, Saul London, and Michael R. Lyu "Achieving Software Quality with Testing Coverage Measures," *IEEE Computer*, Sept. 1994.

8.3.3.10 Test Case Management

If a significant number of test cases is to be run, the management of those runs becomes a significant problem. Tools have been developed to assist in the running of those test cases, and they are collectively referred to as "test case managers."

Test case managers typically are responsible for:

- Test selection. Based on a mapping of test cases vs. program components, the test manager selects those test cases appropriate to a particular run.

- Test execution. The selected test cases are run.

- Test result checking. The results of the test runs are checked against a test oracle, and deviations noted.

- Test report preparation. A summary of the test case successes and failures is prepared.

There is one very special form of test case manager, called an *environment simulator.* This type of manager allows software built to be part of a larger system to be tested in the absence of that system. This is accomplished by building a software product that simulates the large system (the "environment" in which the software is to be run). A test manager then controls interaction between the software under test and the environment simulator program itself, allowing the software under test to perform as it would in the real environment.

For what types of projects are these approaches appropriate? Test managers are useful for large projects, regardless of domain, criticality, or innovativeness. Environment simulators are useful for the real-time, embedded application domain, regardless of project size, criticality, or innovativeness.

8.3.3.11 Test Data Generator

Test data generators are tools that construct test cases. There is a large variety of ways in which that might happen:

- Capturing test cases used before and playing them back for future use (particularly useful where test cases involve repeating a set of online key strokes)

- Selecting portions of "live" databases or files to serve as test cases

- Generating random test cases to fit within specified constraints

- Constructing test cases by examination of software structure to determine what conditions must hold to execute certain segments

The first three techniques are easy to achieve. Off-the-shelf tools are available to create test sets from capture/playback, and from live data files, and/or they may also be easily constructed to fit a project's specific needs. Random generators are also relatively easily constructed to fit a project's needs. (A random number generator must be employed, but most software libraries contain one or more.)

The final technique is still, unfortunately, largely a research concept. Such a tool would be extremely useful for automatically constructing the test cases need to improve structure-driven test coverage, by creating test cases that will execute not-yet-tested portions of a program. But doing so is a complex problem, and there is no off-the-shelf tool available to provide this service at present, although researchers have been working on the concept for a couple of decades or more.

For what types of projects should test case generators be used? Capture/playback is most useful for software with online user interaction, regardless of project size, domain, criticality, or innovativeness. Live data extraction is most useful for data-focused applications, such as business applications. Random generation of test cases is most useful under those circumstances where statistics-driven testing is to be used. Automatic generation of test cases is not sufficiently viable yet that it is recommended for any types of projects. However, should the technique become viable, it would be useful for all projects on which a test coverage analyzer of program logic would be used.

8.3.3.12 Standardized Testing

For certain kinds of applications, there are standard test packages that may be used without needing to construct any new ones. For example, compilers for most leading programming languages can (and must!) be tested using standard sets of test cases focused on the features of the language. Unfortunately, the number of such applications is relatively small.

For what types of projects should standardized testing be employed? For all projects for which such tests are available! However, that is generally limited to certain kinds of systems program applications.

8.3.3.13 Test Documentation

We have already seen from the length of this section of the book that testing can be a complex process. It should be no surprise to the reader to find that it is the most time-consuming portion of the software development process.

That complexity begets the need for documentation. Typical testing documentation includes:

- Test plan. In this document, plans and philosophies for the testing process are detailed, the test cases themselves are included, and a requirements/test case matrix is constructed (showing how requirements-driven coverage will be achieved).

- Test procedure. This document describes how the test cases will be run. It includes a discussion of the facilities needed, the responsibilities of those involved, and the approval process.

- Test report. This document summarizes the results of testing, noting which test cases ran successfully, which did not, and what was done about the latter. Often it is created to describe the results of acceptance testing only and is an exception report, showing what happened only for unusual cases, such as unsuccessful test runs that had to be repeated.

For what types of projects should test case documentation be used? It is especially important for large projects (because it helps get things organized) and for critical ones (because developing documents tends to add rigor to a process). There is no particular domain dependence here, and innovative projects might be less likely to have formal documentation because it is difficult to plan such projects.

8.3.3.14 Test Review

Because the testing process is complex, the process of reviewing testing is also often complex. Test reviews are generally conducted in advance of testing, in order to make sure that the testing to be conducted is necessary and sufficient, and after testing has been completed, to review the test results for acceptance purposes and to record lessons learned. The subject for discussion at these reviews is the test documentation discussed in the previous section.

The types of projects for which test reviews are appropriate matches the types of projects for which testing documentation is appropriate, again as discussed in the preceding section.

8.3.4 TESTING AND VALIDATION SUMMARY

Let us review the requirements of ISO 9000-3, and our own contribution, with respect to testing and validation.

Much of what 9000-3 required was about planning and documenting—what should be present in the test plan, and what should be done during testing.

On the other hand, what we presented in Section 8.3 was considerably more diverse. Here again, we run into the broad spread between "what" and "how." Just as design and implementation were complex technical issues, requiring far more understanding than the simplistic guidance provided by 9000-3, so too, testing and validation need more attention than required by 9000-3 if they are to result in a high quality software product.

There is no reason to disagree with what 9000-3 *does* require—a good quality system will provide specifically for those items it requires. But, we would assert, such a quality system should go considerably further, and we have provided that additional dimension here.

In Table 8.3, we present our recommendations for a more specific testing and validation approach than 9000-3 requires. As with previous summary sections of this book, these recommendations, though deeply felt, are to some extent controversial. If there are patterns to be found in the table, they tend to be these: testing and validation approaches that require tools should often be used only on large or critical projects unless those tools have already been acquired by the organization; and some concepts are advocated elsewhere for testing and validation that are marginally worth considering for any project (e.g., proof of correctness, error seeding, and mutation testing).

Table 8.3 Project Types vs. Techniques: Testing and Validation

Technique/ Tool	Project Type: Size		Application				Criticality		Innovativeness	
	Lg	Sm	Bus	Sci	Sys	R-T	High	Low	High	Low
Desk Checking	Y	Y	Y	Y	Y	Y	Y	Y	Y	Y
Peer Code Review	K	K	K	K	K	K	Y	K	K	K
Structural Analysis	Y	IA	Y	Y	Y	Y	Y	IA	IA	IA
Proof of Correctness	N	N	N	N	N	N	YI	N	N	N
Source Language Debug	Y	Y	Y	Y	Y	Y	Y	Y	Y	Y
Assertion Checker	IA	N	IA	IA	IA	IA	IA	IA	IA	IA
Intentional Failure	N	N	N	N	N	N	N	N	N	N
Performance Analysis	YA	YA	YA	YA	YA	Y	YA	YA	YA	YA
Requirements-Driven Test	100%									
Structure-Driven Test	85%						100%		85%	
Risk-Driven Test	N	N	N	N	N	N	Y	N	N	N
Statistics-Driven Test	YA	N	YA	YA	YA	YA	YI	YA	YA	YA
Test Coverage Analyzer	Use whenever structure-driven testing is used									

Technique/ Tool	Project Type:									
	Size		Application				Criticality		Innovative- ness	
	Lg	Sm	Bus	Sci	Sys	R-T	High	Low	High	Low
Test Case Manage- ment	Y	YA	YA	YA	YA	YA	Y	YA	YA	YA
Test Data Generator	See Section 8.3.3.11 for specifics									
Standard- ized Testing	See Section 8.3.3.12 for specifics									
Test Docu- mentation	Y	N	YA	YA	YA	YA	Y	N	N	YA
Test Review	Y	N	YA	YA	YA	YA	Y	N	N	YA

Legend:
IA = If available
K = Key portions
N = No
Y = Yes
YA = Yes, if applicable
YI = Yes, if all other approaches are also used

8.4 ACCEPTANCE

Once again, it is important to remember here that ISO 9000-3 is oriented toward purchased software. The acceptance process under these circumstances is usually considerably more formal than it is when the software is prepared, for example, for in-house use. Often there is a formal document, prepared in advance, specifying the process of approval (or disapproval) during acceptance testing.

The guidance provided by 9000-3 for acceptance is, once again, minimal:

- The purchaser judges acceptability according to criteria previously agreed upon and by a contractually-defined process.

- Problems will likewise be handled according to pre-established conditions, and will be documented.

- Acceptance test planning shall include a time schedule, evaluation procedures, software/hardware environment/resources, and acceptance criteria.

That is the extent of 9000-3 on acceptance. Like the sections before this, more is needed for a project to conduct successful acceptance tests, although the gap is perhaps not as wide here as in previous sections. In this section, we choose to discuss not only the process of acceptance testing, but the phases of testing that lead up to that testing. Note that in the previous section (on testing and validation), we discussed tools and methods for testing. In this section, we discuss the phases of testing: unit test, integration test, system test, and others. Acceptance testing is only the capstone of an important process that must precede it.

8.4.1 ACCEPTANCE ISSUES

All too often, acceptance is simply a testing process. That is, the customer agrees on a set of tests to be run, and what correct output from those runs will look like. If those tests execute and produce the correct output, the customer signs the appropriate forms and formally takes delivery of the software.

But testing is a necessary, not sufficient, condition for acceptance. The customer taking delivery of the software is taking delivery of all of its quality attributes—its portability, its efficiency, its human engineering, its understandability, its modifiability, and its reliability. That customer is also taking delivery of the software product's documentation.

And all of those aspects of the software product deserve attention at acceptance time.

Testing, it is true, is the most important issue in acceptance, because it is the most critical. If software produces incorrect results, all the rest of its attributes pale into insignificance. And all too often, even with software that has been well scrubbed prior to its acceptance test, bugs pop up in the acceptance process. The software fails to run successfully in the customer's computing environment, or it fails on a surprise test case not among the predictable ones defined in advance.

But there is more to software than its reliability. The acceptance process should address such issues as maintainability, efficiency, how good its user interface is, and if it matters, portability. And certainly it should address the issue of documentation suitability.

Unfortunately, the only way to address these matters is with product inspections. And therein lies the problem that causes this to be an issue. It is rare that the software product is inspected internally at acceptance time. Behavioral tests are common, but inspections are not. There is a reason, of course, why acceptance inspection is rare. The customer taking delivery of the product may not have the skills to do a meaningful inspection at all. But even if they do, software inspection is terribly hard and complex work, with enormous cost involved. It is not surprising that most customers simply run the acceptance tests, examine the user interface, scan the documentation, and assume they have done the job.

For the software producer, of course, this lack of attention at acceptance time is a solution, not a problem! Get the software to pass the acceptance tests, and you are pretty well home free. It is easy to imagine, however, that this condition will not always be true, and as customers get more software street-smart, they may insist on a more thorough acceptance process.

A second issue about acceptance is its degree of formality. It is important to note that much of the 9000-3 text focuses on preparedness and planning. The process of acceptance is to be contractually defined. The pass/fail criteria are defined in advance. Any problems are handled by a pre-established procedure. Prior documentation determines schedules and the acceptance test environment.

The formality of the acceptance process defined in 9000-3 is wise. However, for in-house product delivery, the process will generally be considerably less formal. And although formality tends to eliminate last-minute disagreement, it also tends to beget inflexibility. Remember that, above, we discuss the circumstance where an unexpected test at acceptance time uncovers an unexpected error. The formality of the acceptance process should leave provision for the flexibility of last-minute changes. The last thing a customer wants to discover after acceptance is that they have bought a software product which has been trained to run the acceptance test suite—and nothing else!

8.4.2 UNIT TESTING

Acceptance testing is the culmination of a testing process. By the time the formal acceptance tests are run, the software producers should already know how they are going to come out. They are going to come out successfully because a series of prior tests has been run successfully. Those prior tests start with unit tests.

Unit tests are tests of individual software components, conducted with test drivers that are special code written just to cause the component in question to execute. Unit testing should have been conducted early in the implementation process, with all key components unit-tested even during top-down implementation, and with all components unit-tested if the implementation is bottom-up.

Unit testing has been under attack from a variety of directions. Advocates of formal verification sometimes claim that thorough, mathematical proofs of correctness make them unnecessary. Naive practitioners sometimes claim that software written to be fault-tolerant need not be unit-tested, since the software will recover from failures automatically anyway. Cleanroom advocates say that testing should be removed from the developer (who traditionally does unit testing) and given to independent test groups (who traditionally perform only integration and system testing). Although the disagreements will continue, the bottom line of this book is that it is extremely unwise to curtail unit testing. Its various replacements are unlikely to be as effective in eliminating early software errors as the unit-testing process.

Unit testing is appropriate for all types of projects, no matter their size, domain, criticality, or innovativeness.

8.4.3 INTEGRATION TESTING

Integration testing is the process of putting the software pieces together and seeing how well they play. Recall that in top-down implementation, the integration process is evolutionary—that is, most tests are integration tests of the ever-evolving product—but that in bottom-up testing, integration testing is done all at once (some call it "big bang" testing due to the tendency of the software, when first put together, to blow up—fail—during tests).

If integration tests fail, it is often due to communication errors among the various developers of the various components. An interface was not well understood, or unwarranted assumptions were made by one or more developers—these kinds of problems frequently cause units to test successfully but not play together at integration time.

There is little controversy about integration testing. Typically, integration tests are run by team of developers, those responsible for the components being integrated. Since Cleanroom advocates that developers be separated from all testing, in the Cleanroom process this phase of testing is simply skipped in favor of independent system testing.

Integration testing is appropriate for all types of projects, no matter their size, domain, criticality, or innovativeness. Large projects and critical ones may demand more formality in the process, but the need for some kind of integration testing is independent of the nature of the project.

8.4.4 SYSTEM TESTING

The prior two types of testing are about the software itself. But system testing is about the solution to the problem at hand: does the software correctly perform the functions it was intended to perform in the setting in which they must be performed?

System testing is the first point in the testing process in which the total software product can be examined in a realistic setting. It is here that the acceptance tests, to be run formally later at delivery time, are first executed, (but, of course, system testing must go far beyond the acceptance tests in scope, since acceptance tests typically check only a portion of system capability).

This is also the first point in the testing process at which customers begin to get visibility into the final functioning product. If there are misunderstandings in the requirements—and all too frequently, in the software business, there are—then this is the point at which the customer begins to have the opportunity to exclaim "But that's not what I wanted at all!"

It is this requirements disagreement problem that makes system testing an essential part of software's error removal process. Advocates of formal verification have long suggested, for example, that if software is proven mathematically correct (meaning that it performs the tasks specified by its requirements), that is the severest test of software correctness. But, of course, if the specifications are wrong, then proof of correctness shows us nothing about system correctness—it only shows us that the system is internally consistent with its spec.

Because of that, system testing is a necessary approach for all project types, regardless of size, domain, criticality, or innovativeness. Once again, however, the degree of formality may increase with system size and criticality.

8.4.5 INDEPENDENT TESTING

Software developers, especially those under intense schedule pressures, are probably more anxious to demonstrate that their product is correct than that it is incorrect. But that is a mistake. It is the essence of the testing process that its goal is to find (and subsequently remove) errors, not to avoid finding them.

Because of that tendency, many software enterprises employ something called independent testing. (It is called a variety of names, including product test, but here we use the name that emphasizes the spirit of its intent.) Independent testing is the process of using skilled testers who are not on this product's development team to subject the product to tests. Because independent testers usually get the product to test following integration, this is another form of system test. Independent testers have no emotional investment in whether the software contains errors or not, and in fact are frequently driven by the motivation to find bugs that others have not found.

Independent testing, of course, adds organizational and individual cost to the software project. Because of that, it tends to be most appropriate for large and critical software projects. Innovative projects often involve a smaller number of developers and thus may be less subject to the need for independent testing. Finally, independent testing tends to be independent of domain.

8.4.6 BETA TESTING

With all the preceding testing phases, you would think that software would be ready, following good system testing, including, perhaps, independent testing, for the final and formal acceptance test. But quite commonly it is not.

The problem is that the testers up until this point have

been thinking like software people, not like users. And often users will do things unlike any of the expectations software people may have had for them! That is not a negative comment, necessarily, about users. It may simply mean that contrived data (created by software people) and real data are vastly different.

Because of that, many software producers follow the system test process with a "beta test." In a beta test, the software is released informally to a select set of users, those who know that the software is not yet ready for general release but who are willing to use it (and help debug it) in spite of that fact.

Beta testing tends to be more related to project type than the preceding testing phases. It is especially important for software projects where the product goes into a marketplace. It is also more appropriate for large projects than small ones, and for critical projects than noncritical ones. It tends to be unrelated to project innovativeness.

8.4.7 ACCEPTANCE TESTING

Now we can see why the acceptance test should reach a foregone conclusion! If the preceding testing phases have been performed successfully, there is little excuse for the formal test to fail. Commonly, the acceptance test has been run many times at system test (and perhaps independent test) before the software product comes up for acceptance.

The acceptance test has already been thoroughly discussed in the preceding material. It only remains to be said here that acceptance testing is wise for all projects, but the degree of formality may rise substantially for large projects and critical ones. In the least formal form of acceptance testing, the customer may simply witness system testing. Sometimes innovative projects, especially those whose nature is exploratory, may not need any acceptance test at all.

8.4.8 ACCEPTANCE SUMMARY

Let us review what 9000-3 requires for acceptance. As we saw in Section 8.4, the requirements are about planning the acceptance process sufficiently that these things are defined before the acceptance test occurs: acceptance criteria, acceptance process, failure options and process, documentation requirements, time schedule, evaluation procedures, and software, hardware, and environment resources.

Once again, the process we describe in this section is considerably more elaborate than that required by ISO 9000-3. In this section, we have seen acceptance as the culmination of a planned sequence of interim test processes, conducted such that—if all goes well—the acceptance test is an anticlimax.

Nevertheless, it is important to stress the wisdom of the 9000-3 requirement for planning the acceptance process. Anyone who has ever gone through an acceptance—whether it was successful or not, but especially if it was not—can speak for the value of up-front planning and predefined agreements. It is difficult enough when an acceptance test fails, for example, without having to invent the process for dealing with it on the spot.

Table 8.4 summarizes what activities should be conducted on which types of projects. You will note that most types of projects call for most types of activities. The process of testing is one that should not be skimped on; the result of such skimping is usually unreliable software, and unreliable software is often worse than no software at all. The only exceptions to the requirement for most activities to support most project types is for small projects. There, some of the intermediate phases of testing may be skipped (or may not even exist; for example, there may be nothing to integration test on a small project) as long as there is a comprehensive test at the end of the phased testing process. Even under those circumstances, note that it is unwise to eliminate the up-front testing (unit test) and the final testing (acceptance test).

Table 8.4 Project Types vs. Techniques: Acceptance

Technique/ Tool	Project Type:									
	Size		Application				Criticality		Innovative-ness	
	Lg	Sm	Bus	Sci	Sys	R-T	High	Low	High	Low
Unit Test	Y	Y	Y	Y	Y	Y	Y	Y	Y	Y
Integration Test	Y	N	Y	Y	Y	Y	Y	Y	Y	Y
System Test	Y	N	Y	Y	Y	Y	Y	Y	Y	Y
Independent Test	Y	N	Y	Y	Y	Y	Y	Y	?	Y
Beta Test	Y	?	Y	Y	Y	Y	Y	Y	Y	Y
Acceptance Test	Y	Y?	Y	Y	Y	Y	Y	Y	Y	Y

Legend:
Y = Yes
? = Depends on circumstances
N = No

8.5 REPLICATION, DELIVERY, AND INSTALLATION

Of all the phases of software development, this is the least taxing. It is in this phase, and only this phase, that most of software's work is mechanistic.

What is particularly interesting about this fact is that this is the phase which, for most other disciplines, would be one of the more complex. It is in this phase for more traditional products that manufacturing occurs. But software requires no manufacture, and so the replication part of this phase consists simply of duplication. Delivery media (commonly disk) copies of the software product are made by standard file duplication processes.

Delivery and installation are a bit more complicated, but

not much. Delivery is simply shipment, and since the media on which the software is shipped is light and small, there is little cost or complexity to shipment. A manifest detailing the contents of the media should be created to accompany the shipment, but that, too, is relatively simple. Installation is more complicated, in that installation procedures must be carefully documented and exactly followed.

ISO 9000-3 is fairly specific in its requirements for this phase, perhaps because these standards were originated for more traditional products and then transferred to be applied to software. (It is interesting that what 9000-3 has to say about these simple processes is roughly the same length as what it has to say about much more cognitive and complex software tasks!)

Regarding replication, 9000-3 requires:

- Consideration of the number of copies to be made, the type of media to be used, the provision of the necessary documentation, and a statement of the copyright and licensing terms of acquisition

- Consideration of the custody of master and back-up copies of the product, including disaster recovery plans

- Consideration of the period for which the supplier is obligated to supply copies

Regarding delivery, 9000-3 is quite terse:

- Provision should be made for verifying the correctness and completeness of the delivered copies.

Regarding installation, 9000-3 requires:

- The roles, responsibilities, and obligations of the purchaser and supplier should be clearly established, taking into account schedule, facilities access, availability of skilled personnel, a validation procedure, and a formal approval procedure.

For this phase, the requirements of 9000-3 are nearly sufficient. There is little need to elaborate on them in this section. For those interested in any additional detail, a standard format for documentation for this phase, the "Version Description Document," is provided in [Glass 1988, p. 140]. (It is a U.S. Department of Defense standard for delivery documentation.)

There are, however, a couple of issues concerning this phase.

Reference

[Glass 1988] Robert L. Glass, *Software Communication Skills*, Englewood Cliffs, N.J.: Prentice Hall.

8.5.1 REPLICATION, DELIVERY, AND INSTALLATION ISSUES

One of the tasks software people do least well is to document what they have done. Documentation is often skimpy, laden with "computerese," and poorly written. Because software documentation is so poor, a whole industry of book publishers specializing in "how-to" computer books has sprung up, filling the gap software people apparently were unable to fill.

In this phase that problem is common. Delivery manifests are particularly problematic; it is often difficult to tell, from the meager documentation that accompanies a delivery, what the media contains and why. The task of writing this documentation is not complex; it is probably given short shrift due to the crush of time at the end of a project, rather than done badly because it is difficult to do.

Installation instructions, by contrast, are usually sufficient for a reasonably mentally well-endowed person to follow. That is probably because without usable installation instructions, the delivery is pointless: the product cannot be used.

The other issue surrounding replication, delivery, and installation is legal. For peculiar historical reasons, the purchaser of software may or may not own the software for which they have paid, and may or may not have the right to make copies of it. It is important during product negotiations to pin down ownership, of both the software (including all libraries) and the products necessary to replicate it. If the software is custom-built, that is a matter for negotiation between the seller and purchaser. If software is purchased as a package, that is another matter—custom at present dictates that the purchaser is not truly an owner, and has no right to make copies. Because the legalities of software purchase are so counterintuitive, it is especially important to pin down all details about these matters well before replication, delivery, and installation.

8.5.2 POSTDELIVERY REVIEW

There is one topic connected to this phase of software development that *does* deserve elaboration. At the time the project has been completed, and delivery consummated, it is typical in the software business to free the developers to move on to other projects. That practice is a mistake.

There is one last, vitally important, task for the development team. Now is the time, with the pressure of schedule removed, to think back over the project and contemplate what went right and what went wrong. It is time to capture lessons learned [IEEE 1993]. This practice is called a variety of names, but our favorite is "postdelivery review." (It seems particularly better than "postmortem review," another popular name!)

There are two facets to a postdelivery review, that associated with the product and that associated with the development process.

- A product review should be held to consider reactions to the delivered system, with customers and users participating actively, and developers being eager listeners. If the product has been found to be only marginally similar to what the customer/user really wanted, now is the time to figure out how to fix that and how to avoid that problem next time. There is usually a delay between actual delivery and the conducting of this review, to give the users time to find out what the product *really* does for them. Some recommend that this review be held 3 to 12 months after delivery. Following the review, it is important to document its lessons learned, and set action items for employing them.

• Because the construction of software is such a complex process, it is often true that the experience of developing a software system is different each time. New mistakes are made, and new and better ways of doing things are discovered. It is important that those lessons be not only learned but documented, so that good approaches can be reused on future projects and bad ones avoided. If quantitative data is kept on software projects—and we strongly advocate the use of such metrics—then this is the time when the numbers should be run one last time, analyzed, and conclusions drawn. Probably the most comprehensive approach for recording these kinds of findings is "The Experience Factory" concept, developed at NASA-Goddard with the assistance of the University of Maryland Computer Science Department and Computer Sciences Corp. [Basili 1992]. This sort of review must happen almost immediately after product delivery, since the team usually disperses quite quickly at project conclusion. (Note that one design requirement of ISO 9000-3, having to do with capturing design lessons learned, is directly related to this process.)

References

[Basili 1992] "The Software Engineering Laboratory: An Operational Software Experience Factory," *Proc. Int'l. Conf. on Software Engineering*, Los Alamitos,CA: IEEE CS Press, 1992.

[IEEE 1993] Special issue on "Lessons Learned," *IEEE Software*, Sept. 1993.

8.5.3 REPLICATION, DELIVERY, AND INSTALLATION SUMMARY

It is easy to summarize the impact of ISO 9000-3 on this process. A project quality plan should explicitly satisfy all of the requirements of the standard (listed in section 8.5), and since that is not particularly difficult to do we do not expand on what 9000-3 offers. We do add one task, however, which is connected to an earlier 9000-3 requirement. We suggest the employment of two different kinds of post-delivery reviews, one about the product and involving customers and users, and one about the process and involving only developers. The need for such reviews is largely independent of project type; perhaps small projects would treat the postdelivery review less formally than other projects. Innovative projects may or may not involve replication, delivery, and installation. Whether they do or not, however, the postdelivery review is particularly important to capture what may be unique lessons learned (about the subject of the innovation).

8.6 MAINTENANCE

Here again, the fact that ISO 9000-3 is oriented toward contractually purchased software becomes significant. For example, the first requirement of 9000-3 is that there be a maintenance plan that is "defined and agreed upon beforehand by the supplier and purchaser." Although in the past such maintenance plans were uncommon, they are becoming the norm for both contractual and in-house software projects, and for contractual projects they are particularly vital.

Let us look at what 9000-3 requires for software maintenance:

- A maintenance plan, to include
  - Scope of maintenance
  - Identification and initial status of product
  - Maintenance activities
    - (use same procedures as development)
    - resolve problems
    - modify interfaces
    - functional expansion or performance improvement
  - Maintenance records and reports
    - problem report lists, showing:
      - responsible organization
      - change priority
      - result of corrective action
      - statistical data on errors and changes
    - release reports
      - ground rules regarding the role of patches
      - descriptions of the types (or classes) of release
      - provision for informing the purchaser of change plans
      - provision for regression testing methods
      - provision for multisite maintenance
- (Optional) definition of a maintenance support organization
  - Representatives from both supplier and purchaser
  - Perform (flexible) planning
  - Identify facilities and resources

As can be seen here, much of what ISO 9000-3 requires is about planning and documentation. For the most part, there is nothing wrong with what ISO 9000-3 demands. The major problem here is that what ISO 9000-3 requires does not begin to describe what is necessary during the maintenance phase to maintain a high-quality software product. The gap between necessary and sufficient seems even larger here than it was in the previous life cycle phases.

8.6.1 MAINTENANCE ISSUES

Maintenance is a particularly interesting case in the overall context of software engineering. Traditionally, it has been underresearched and poorly understood by academics. In spite of the fact that there is near-unanimous agreement that maintenance is the biggest cost driver in software, there are few of the following:

- Maintenance methodologies

- Maintenance CASE tools

- Maintenance theories

- Maintenance courses in academe

A great deal of what is written about maintenance is at best confused and at worst wrong. For example, a few years ago it was common to find people talking about "eliminating maintenance," as if it were a bad thing. But quite early in the history of software engineering we learned that maintenance is predominantly about making changes to the software product, not about fixing errors. Roughly 60% of maintenance cost is about change, and only 17% is about correction. The remaining 23% is about adaptation (to an evolving infrastructure environment) and the ever-popular "other." Clearly, with this data in mind, it is neither necessary nor even desirable to eliminate maintenance. The softness of a software problem solution allows it to be changed more easily than the products of other disciplines; clearly, far from being a problem, maintenance is a solution, a powerful capability that software offers which its competitive disciplines do not!

Thus, it is fair to say that the most common problem, and therefore the most important issue, in software maintenance is *ignorance*. Here is a case where most software professionals know at least something about maintenance (it is commonly the place where new hires are assigned, for example), but few academics and researchers do. Although a few instances of software maintenance research are being performed, such instances are rare. Worse yet, some of the research that *is* being performed springs from the minds of the researchers rather than from the rich history of software maintenance in practice. Until researchers learn to build software maintenance research on a platform of empirical study, taking advantage of the decades of knowledge in industry, research progress will be both slow and faulty.

As an example of the ignorance discussed above, consider this: the list of maintenance activities found in ISO 9000-3 does not encompass a list of software maintenance tasks published as far back as 1979. In that list, we see that maintenance is a sequence of these events:

1. Define and understand the change to be made.

2. Review the maintenance documentation.

3. Trace the relevant program logic.

4. Make the change.

5. Test the change.

6. Update the maintenance documentation.

To ensure that software quality is kept during the maintenance process, consideration must be given to each of these events. Fortunately, most of them are similar to the events in the software development life cycle. Note that event 1 is about requirements, 3 is about reversing the design and coding activity, 4 is about coding, and 5 is about testing. Only events 2 and 6, having to do with maintenance documentation, and 3, which is a reversal of the development process, are clearly different between the maintenance events and the development phases. Because of that, one would expect emphasis to be placed, in maintenance considerations, on the subjects of documentation and reverse design and coding.

Unfortunately, that is rarely the case. Lip service is paid to the subject of maintenance documentation, but it is rarely produced in practice and rarely discussed in research. We will return to this subject in a later section of this chapter. Reverse design and coding activities have finally caught the eye of the software research community, and the topics of "Reverse engineering, restructuring, and re-engineering" suddenly became popular in the early 1990s. However, too much of that research treatment is naive. That topic, too, we will return to later in this chapter.

The neglect of software maintenance followed by its "discovery" early in this decade has led to the plague with which the software community is often inflicted regarding new ideas, *hype*. Hype is the second big contemporary issue in software maintenance. It is common, now that people understand the importance of, for example, reverse engineering, to find that researchers say they are making progress toward automating it, vendors claim to already have automation tools in the marketplace, and managers buy these tools and spend huge amounts of money. As with most other hyped ideas, however, reality runs a distant second to the promises, and much more is being promised than is being achieved.

Fortunately, in spite of this ignorance and hype, some progress is being made in our ability to perform maintenance. That (real) progress is the subject of the next few sections of this chapter.

8.6.2 PREVENTIVE MAINTENANCE

In the best of all possible worlds, good maintenance begins with good development; that is, a software product will be much more maintainable if it is built originally with maintenance in mind. This patently obvious statement is, unfortunately, rarely supported by what is actually done during development in the practice of software. Instead, maintenance is treated as tomorrow's problem, and its impacts are usually ignored in the world of today.

There are several reasons for this. The oldest reason is that software is such a complex problem that getting it to work today seems too difficult a problem to be further complicated by the needs of change tomorrow. The newest reason is that software is built to such impossible schedules that there is never enough time for today's tasks, let alone tomorrow's. Both of these reasons—all of these reasons—are insufficient. The incremental cost of building maintainable software is so small that there are, in reality, few valid reasons for not doing it. And the savings of building software that is maintainable vs. building software that is not are so clear that the cost/benefit figures are awesome.

What should the developer do to produce maintainable software? We answer that question with two notions, single-point control and defensive programming.

8.6.2.1 Single-Point Control

If something is to be done nearly identically at several places in a software product, it should be done in one place that is referenced from the other places. With this centralization of capability comes the maintainability advantage that changes to that "something to be done" can be made in one place, rather than running the risk of doing it inconsistently in several places.

Single-point control translates into so many software concepts that it is almost magical in its properties: modular design and code, data abstraction, object orientation (including inheritance), table-driven (and file-driven) design and code, and structured documentation. Given the powerful advocacy of the supporters of each of these individual concepts, the generalization offered by single-point control should be software's most-advocated concept! It is important that the single point of control be an intrinsic part of the problem and/or its solution, not a cosmetic part. For example, a repeated key problem *task* or solution *function* or *object* would be a candidate, whereas two similar data structures used for different purposes which might diverge over time should not.

8.6.2.2 Defensive Programming

In a software engineering world short of disciplinary principles, single-point control may be the most important. Closely behind this lies another preventive maintenance concept, "defensive programming." Defensive programming is about anticipation, building a software product so that it will continue to live on no matter what the future holds in store for it.

Defensive programming is a collection of concepts whose goal is to ward off future, maintenance-time problems:

- Exception handling, the notion that the software must handle unexpected as well as expected circumstances with aplomb (usually about rare but foreseen situations)

- Assertions, the notion of the software dynamically checking its own function and reacting if something has gone wrong (about largely unforeseen situations)

- Diagnostic readiness, the notion of leaving built-in debug code in the production version of a product so that it can be invoked by a command from a problem investigator to produce diagnostic output without need for product recompilation

- Margins, the notion that software should be built with more capacity (in both space and time) than is immediately needed to facilitate maintenance-time growth

- Audit trails, the notion that the software should record (in cockpit recorder fashion) a record of its behavior so that if a crash happens the causes can be reconstructed

- Complexity limitation, the notion that certain programming practices add unwarranted complexity to solutions (e.g., deep nesting or the uncontrolled use of GOTOs) and should be avoided

- Limits on unsafe practices, the notion that certain programming practices are inherently unsafe (doing mixed-data type operations, for example) and yet—rarely—necessary (about allowing unsafe practices to be used only if they are explicitly announced and justified to management by the programmer who uses them)

- Fault tolerance, the notion that the software will dynamically recover from any unexpected crises (discussed in an earlier chapter of this book)

8.6.3 DOCUMENTATION

Here is a task with very little controversy that represents one of the biggest problems in software maintenance. Documentation to support maintenance is accepted by everyone as important to the maintenance process, but almost no one produces it.

Why is this so? The answer comes from one technologist foible and one management foible:

- The technologist foible is that the creation of software documentation is one of the least interesting tasks of software development. Most developers simply hate to write, and the level of detail needed in good maintenance documentation makes it the least interesting of those uninteresting documentation tasks.

- The management foible is that most projects today are managed by schedule, a schedule which is usually ambitious and frequently unachievable, and maintenance documentation is the biggest piece of baggage that is jettisoned in an attempt to recoup from schedule problems.

Coupling these two foibles means that software maintenance documentation rarely gets done. That seems especially ironic because:

- 50–80% or more of the cost of software lies in maintenance.

- Everyone agrees that maintenance documentation is vital to doing good maintenance.

The problem of maintenance documentation is not one of knowledge, but one of will. What is needed is simple: a straightforward requirement that no software product will go into maintenance without a reviewed and accepted maintenance document accompanying it, with a follow-on commitment to keep that documentation up to date once maintenance begins.

But it is possible to attack the foibles problem with some wisdom. A minimalist approach to good maintenance documentation should include these concepts:

- A top-level document, containing:
  - Overall product design
    - logic structure
    - data structure
  - A hierarchic collection of middle-level design views, sufficient to relate the top level to the bottom level
  - Pointers to the places where the bottom-level is documented
  - Design issues: history, rationale, and philosophy

- Bottom-level documentation, consisting of:
  - Commentary in the source, showing:
    - logic structure and meaning

- data structure and meaning
- code anomalies
  - Readable source, including:
    - structured, indented code
    - meaningful naming conventions
- A procedure for ensuring that maintenance documentation will be kept up to date as the product itself is changed. (Without this proviso, it is not worth doing maintenance documentation at all. In those few cases where software maintenance documentation *does* exist today, it is frequently out of date, and thus unusable, because maintainers have not changed the documentation as they changed the product.)

It is interesting that ISO 9000-3 says virtually nothing about maintenance documentation. That is particularly odd since the essence of what it advocates in general is documentation and more documentation (one writer on ISO 9000 says, "When in doubt, document"). This is symptomatic of the underlying problem of the standard—it goes through the motions of creating a quality approach, but fails to come to grips with the essence of what software quality is really all about.

8.6.4 CODE ANALYZERS

With this section, we change gears. We are moving from those things that should be done during development to facilitate maintenance—we called them "preventive maintenance"—to those things that are done during maintenance.

There was a time when there was very little to say about the process of doing maintenance. Maintainers did it, and usually did so successfully, but without much understanding of the overall process in which they were engaged. Fortunately, that has changed. The change is no more apparent than in the emergence and use of techniques and tools to support maintenance. In this section and the next several, we present a class of techniques and tools to assist in the maintenance process.

The first class of tools we refer to generically as "code analyzers." Recall that in Section 8.6 we presented a list of the tasks of maintenance. Two of the more important of those tasks were "trace the relevant program logic" and "make the change." Code analyzers are tools to help with those tasks.

Code analyzer tools come in several varieties, and we will discuss each of those varieties in turn:

Cross-reference/browser: These tools help the maintainer understand interrelationships in the code, answering such questions as "from where is module xyz called?" or "where do we use variable abc?" If a change is to be made involving a module or a variable, it is vital to ask and answer such questions.

Call structure generator: These tools help the maintainer understand the overall logic structure of the code. A well-modularized software product often contains a hierarchical (some would say networked) collection of modules calling other modules. If a change is to be made in a lower-level module, it is important to find which high-level modules it affects. If, for some reason, modules need to be grouped (to make paging more efficient, for example), it is vital to group together those modules which are interrelated by call structure.

Performance analyzer: These tools help the maintainer identify which parts of the software product are consuming unwarranted amounts of time. Their use is a prelude to addressing the inefficiencies of those parts.

Metrics analyzer: These tools help the maintainer identify which parts of the software product are highly complex. Their use is a prelude to addressing the complexity of those parts.

Code auditor: These tools help the maintainer identify areas of the code that fail to conform to standards. (Note that we have already seen that automated tools cannot identify a large portion of standards violations. A certain amount of code auditing must be manual.)

Requirements tracers: These tools help the maintainer follow the linkage between a top-level requirement and the parts of the as-built product (including documentation and test cases) that result from it, or vice versa. Their use is a prelude to determining whether a portion of code must change when a requirement changes. Unfortunately, most such tools today are not as effective as one would like, partially because of the "requirements explosion" discussed earlier in this book.

8.6.5 DATA ANALYZERS

A second class of maintenance support concepts is data analyzers. Just as code analyzers support the understanding of code and its logic, data analyzers support the understanding of the data. They are useful for the same maintenance activities—tracing the program logic and making the change—as are code analyzers. If a project employs data-oriented design (or perhaps even object-oriented design), then this type of concept may be more important than the code analyzer.

Just as code analyzers come in several varieties, so do data analyzers.

Data layout: These tools help the maintainer see the overall data organization in graphic form.

Data name standardization: These tools help the maintainer re-organize the software's name structure to be more consistent and meaningful.

Data extraction: These tools help the maintainer obtain small data collections from bigger, often "live," collections for such purposes as creating test cases.

Data normalization: These tools help the maintainer standardize a database to fit the database's rules.

8.6.6 CHANGE ANALYZERS

A third class of support concept is change analyzers. Change analyzers focus on the task of making the change, once the code to be changed is sufficiently well understood.

Change analyzers come in several varieties:

Comparator: The comparator is a tool that performs file comparison. It is especially useful for determining the places in which one version of a software product differs from another version. By using the comparator, it is possible to review actual changes made against the changes that were intended to be made. (The comparator is also useful for comparing current test case file output against a test oracle.)

Change tracker: The change tracker is a clerical/managerial tool for reporting the content and status of software changes.

Documentation manager: The documentation manager is a tool that assists in the production of updated software documentation. It provides such services as marking changed material with change bars so that readers can quickly see what is new between the previous version of the document and a new one.

8.6.7 CONSTRUCTORS

A fourth class of support concepts is constructors. Constructors help with the "rebuilding the system" portion of the "make the change" maintenance task.

Constructors also come in several varieties:

Conditional compilation: The conditional compiler is a tool that assists in the maintenance of multiple versions of a software product in one configuration. The conditional compiler is executed immediately before compilation to select the particular version to be compiled from the multiple versions available.

Reformatter: The reformatter is a tool that takes a badly indented and white-spaced source code and reformats it to meet format standards. (It is sometimes referred to as a "prettyprinter".) Note that reformatters destroy the programmer's original format in favor of a standard, which may or may not be a positive change. Because of that, some reformatters allow programmer or organizational specification of the format to be used.

Restructurer: The restructurer is a tool that takes a badly structured source code and reformats it to meet structured coding conventions.

Configuration management/version control: These tools help prevent the loss of a software product by organizing a collection of backups from which any "lost" version can be reconstructed. They also help keep track of these multiple versions and backups.

Translator: These tools translate from one source code to another. They are used for a variety of purposes, such as to upgrade old source code to a new variant of the same language, to assist in changing a program from one source language to another (e.g., COBOL to C++), or to convert a program from a very high-level language for which there is no compiler support to a compilable language.

8.6.8 TESTERS

A final class of support concepts is testers. Testers assist in the "test the change" task of software maintenance. Most test tools are the same as those applied during development (those will not be discussed below); therefore, only one maintenance test concept will be described here.

Regression testing: Regression testing is a concept that may or may not be supported by specific tools. When a program is changed during maintenance, more than simply the intended impact of the change must be tested. It is also important to make sure that program functionality supposedly not effected by the change has not, indeed, been effected. Regression testing is the notion of reusing a collection of known test cases with a correct test oracle against each new version of the software product to make sure that the changes have not dislodged anything that ought to work.

This concludes the several sections of this chapter on maintenance support concepts. Many of these concepts are supported by tools currently available in the software marketplace. To relate a concept to the specific tools that support it, refer to any periodically published software tools catalog, such as *Guide to Software Productivity Aids,* published by Applied Computer Research, Box 82266, Phoenix, AZ 85071.

8.6.9 CHANGE REVIEW AND REPORTING

Changing the software product during maintenance is more than a matter of receiving user requests and making changes. There are decisions to be made about if and when to make changes; there are reports to be produced showing status of change requests received. The intent of these processes is to manage, and communicate about, maintenance changes.

Change review is usually handled by a board with the authority to decide what changes to make, which ones not to make, and what priority should be assigned to those to be made. The organizational level of the change review board may be anywhere from purely technical (user + maintainer) to extremely high-level (the NASA Space Shuttle program, for example, which in the 1990s is only about product change, handles change review at the highest levels of management), with all the organizational-level stops in between.

Change reporting is generally supported by a generalized or special-purpose tool that tracks change board decisions, maintainer progress in implementing changes, and changes vs. released versions. The change report can be used to check the status of a particular change, and to show trends in changes.

8.6.10 THE R-WORDS: REVERSE ENGINEERING AND RE-ENGINEERING

In recent years, as the inevitable increasing interest in software maintenance has finally occurred, that interest has manifested itself around a collection of buzzwords, all beginning with the letter R. Those buzzwords are, typically:

- Reverse engineering—the act of examining a software product in order to figure out how it works

- Re-engineering—the act of changing a software product to make it better, usually to make it more maintainable and not because of any particular change request

- Restructuring—the act of converting unstructured code into structured code

- Reuse—the act of using previously built concepts or components in a current software project

In this section, we will only discuss two of those terms. We will not discuss restructuring, because it was already covered under "change analyzers," and because it is small potatoes compared to the other R-word concepts. (That is, the task of restructuring is automatable, and has considerably less impact on the worth of a software product than do the other R-words). We will not discuss reuse because, although it is an extremely important concept, it is only peripherally related to maintenance. (That is, although it is possible to scour previously built software to identify concepts that can be reused, it is probably better to think reuse during development and build generalized, reusable code at that time.)

That leaves us with reverse engineering and re-engineering. Why do we single them out here for special treatment?

Reverse engineering is important because it is an umbrella term that covers much of what is complex and difficult about software maintenance. Referring back to the tasks of software maintenance in Section 8.6, it is clear from prior studies that one task of maintenance is more time-consuming than any other. That task is understanding the existing software in order to make the change, characterized in the task list as "review the maintenance documentation" and "trace the relevant program logic." Reverse engineering is the hot-button buzzword for this very old software concept. In doing reverse engineering, we seek to understand how and why the software product does what it does.

It is particularly important to point out that reverse engineering, in this sense, is *not* goal-oriented. In the definition of the term, we have said nothing about *why* we might reverse engineer. Most commonly, we reverse engineer in order to document how the software functions (creating maintenance documentation after the development is complete), or in order to make a specific change to the software.

But there is another reason to reverse engineer. That reason involves understanding the software in order to identify portions of it that are hard to understand or work with and should be changed simply to make understanding easier. And that is where the final R-word, re-engineering, comes into play. This form of reverse engineering is a prelude to re-engineering, where re-engineering is the act of changing the software product simply to make it more maintainable.

Note that some confusing ambiguity has occurred as the term re-engineering gained prominence. It has been preempted into another buzzword, "business process re-engineering," which is largely not about software at all, but about ways of improving an enterprise's functioning in order to make it more effective and efficient (although sometimes business process re-engineering can be facilitated, or must be facilitated, by building software consistent with the newly re-engineered business process).

It should be noted that reverse engineering and re-engineering are largely intellectual processes, only marginally supported (and supportable) by tools. It would not be necessary to make this statement except that, in the excess of excitement that surrounds any new buzzword, there have been implications that automated reverse engineering and re-engineering are possible. Certain code analyzer and data analyzer tools (see Sections 8.6.4 and 8.6.5) may help us do reverse engineering, and may pave the way for re-engineering, but they do *not* automate those activities.

8.6.11 MAINTENANCE SUMMARY

Let us review what 9000-3 requires for maintenance.

There is a great deal of planning-oriented material required by ISO 9000-3, in the form of a fairly elaborate maintenance plan, to contain definitions of scope, activities, records/reports, and support organizations.

And that is it. The presumption here is that if you plan maintenance well, you will do it well.

But maintenance is, more than any other phase of software, about expecting the unexpected. Just as home remodeling is full of surprises, as the remodeler tears the wall surfaces away from the house's structure in order to see what work is *really* needed, so it is with software maintenance. It is difficult to know in advance how complicated a particular change will be. If a change is, for example, outside the scope of the original design envelope of the software product, then making that change will be extremely difficult, if not impossible. And gaining visibility into that original design envelope is just as complicated as anticipating the structure of a house before the wall surfaces are removed. It is for this reason that planning of maintenance is a complex and frustrating process. Certainly planning is possible, but it may be difficult to carry out the plans unless they are abysmally simplistic, just because it is difficult to anticipate what is difficult about maintenance. Because of that, maintenance planning is more often about the use of methods and tools than about anticipating the structure of the product.

Nevertheless, in order to achieve ISO 9000-3 certification, it is necessary to prepare this kind of plan. It is important to bear in mind, however, that much more than the plan is needed if quality maintenance is going to be performed on a quality software product.

Ironically, probably the most important need of the maintainer is suitable maintenance documentation. It is ironic because, for all of the 9000-3 emphasis on various kinds of documentation, nothing specific is said about this kind of document. Previously we have said that 9000-3 provides necessary but not sufficient advice on doing quality software work. Here, it becomes increasingly uncomfortable even to say "necessary," and "sufficient" is far away indeed.

Table 8.5 summarizes what maintenance techniques should be applied to the various kinds of software projects. The most noticeable thing about the table is that most types of projects demand most techniques. The only exceptions tend to be small projects, where the tool-oriented techniques should only be used if they are already available (because small projects typically cannot justify procurement of a tool just for their needs), and innovative projects, where it is possible that, depending on the findings of the project, little or no maintenance may be necessary.

Why should most types of maintenance techniques be applied to most types of projects? Because maintenance is ubiquitous. Most projects, regardless of size or domain or criticality or innovativeness, require maintenance following development. The more successful the project, the more maintenance is needed (because maintenance, as you may recall, is largely about change, and customers/users don't bother to change software that doesn't approach their needs—they discard it).

Table 8.5 Project Types vs. Techniques: Maintenance

Technique/ Tool	Project Type:									
	Size		Application				Criticality		Innovative- ness	
	Lg	Sm	Bus	Sci	Sys	R-T	High	Low	High	Low
Preventive Mainte- nance	Y	Y	Y	Y	Y	Y	Y	Y	Y?	Y
Documenta- tion	Y	N	Y	Y	Y	Y	Y	Y	Y?	Y
Code Ana- lyzers	Y	IA	Y	Y	Y	Y	Y	IA	IA	Y
Data Ana- lyzers	Y	IA	Y	Y?	Y?	Y?	Y	IA	IA	Y
Change Analyzers	Y	IA	Y	Y	Y	Y	Y	IA	IA	Y
Construc- tors	Y	IA	Y	Y	Y	Y	Y	IA	IA	Y
Testers	Y	IA	Y	Y	Y	Y	Y	IA	IA	Y
Change Review and Reporting	Y	IA	Y	Y	Y	Y	Y	Y	IA	Y
Reverse engineering	Y	Y	Y	Y	Y	Y	Y	Y	Y	Y
Re-engi- neering	IN	IN	IN	IN	IN	IN	IN	IN	IN	IN

Legend:
IA = If available (don't procure for this project alone)
IN - If needed
N = No
Y = Yes
Y? = Probably yes

8.7 SUPPORTING ACTIVITIES

ISO 9000-3 identifies a number of supporting activities, those software activities that are independent of life-cycle phase. They are configuration management, document control, quality records, measurement, "rules, practices and conventions," tools and techniques, purchasing, "included software product," and training. To each of these supporting activities, it devotes several paragraphs of discussion:

1. *Configuration management.* This activity should:

   • Identify versions, components, build status, and changes

   • Control multi-person product updates

   • Coordinate multi-version products

   In addition, there should be a configuration management plan, defining: organizational responsibilities; tasks and activities; tools, techniques, and methodologies; and when during the project configuration management is to begin.

   Those things to be controlled are to include specifications, tools, interfaces, documents, computer files, and changes. For released products, there should be procedures to facilitate traceability.

2. *Document control.* This activity should control the quality system document, planning documents, and product documents (development phase inputs and outputs, verification and validation plans and results, user/purchaser documentation, and maintenance documentation). Control should consist of determining which documents specifically are to be controlled, approving and issuing control procedures, and defining change procedures. Following that, document control should ensure that the controlled documents are available where needed, and that obsolete documents are purged. Document change

control is also to be employed: responsible organizations identified, a master list and control procedure identified, and the conditions for reissue identified.

3. *Quality records.* This activity is responsible for defining and keeping records of quality activities, showing achievement of the required quality and effective operation of the quality system. Retention time is to be defined, provision made for minimizing deterioration, and records are to be readily retrieved.

4. *Measurement.* This activity is responsible for collecting product and process metrics. However, 9000-3 is not very specific on what those metrics should be, instead noting that "there are currently no universally accepted measures of software quality." The only specific type of metric to be collected is defect metrics.

   The purpose of the measurement is to be, from a *product* point of view, to identify current levels of performance, to support undertaking remedial actions, and to help establish specific improvement goals. *Process* metrics should be about process success vs. milestones and schedules, and the role of the process in reducing fault introduction and providing early fault detection.

   Finally, the measurement section of 9000-3 says some fairly nonspecific things about establishing measurement rules, and about using tools, facilities, and techniques to facilitate measurement.

5. *Rules, practices, and conventions.* This activity is to provide those rules, practices, and conventions needed to make ISO 9000-3 work. That is essentially all 9000-3 says!

6. *Tools and techniques.* This activity simply says that the supplier should use tools and techniques to assist in making a quality product, for both product development and management purposes. It also says that improvements to tools and techniques may be made as required.

7. *Purchasing.* This activity is responsible for defining what happens if the *supplier* needs to purchase a product or service in order to deliver the software product. The tasks to be performed include providing a clear description of what is to be purchased, defining the needed requirements, maintaining appropriate records on the purchase, and conducting appropriate validation efforts. The purchase choice is to be based on the subcontractor's ability to meet the purchase requirements.

8. *Included software product.* This activity is similar to "purchasing," above, but with a slight twist. It is about the need of the supplier to include, in the product being produced, software from the *purchaser* or a third party. The relevant section of 9000-3 is quite short; it requires that the supplier establish and maintain procedures for validation, storage, protection, and maintenance of the included product. Provision for maintenance of the included product, and/or rejection of an unsuitable included product, must also be made.

9. *Training.* This activity is about training the supplier personnel who are producing the product. 9000-3 requires that the supplier establish and maintain procedures for defining training needs and conducting training. Such training could be about tools, techniques, and methodologies; the application domain for which the software is being built; or the management of the software activities.

8.7.1 SUPPORTING ACTIVITY ISSUES

The biggest issue surrounding these supporting activities is when a project should do what. It is popular in the software world of the 1990s to say that all projects should use all approaches to software construction. But, as you will recall from earlier in this book, there are others who respond with derision to this "one size fits all" approach.

The problem here is that many of these supporting activities can take on grandiose lives of their own. Configuration management, for example, although vitally important and relatively simple in concept, is the subject of 400+-page books, whole elaborate organizational structures, and mind-numbing controls on some software projects. When should configuration management be formal and elaborate, and when should it be informal and simple?

The same thing is true of lots of other supporting activities. ISO 9000-3 speaks of change and document control, for example. Should these be the responsibility of multiperson groups with hierarchic management structures, or should they be tasks to be assumed by the development team along with the other vital activities they are doing?

Perhaps the most controversial of these activities is the quality control organization. Although this material in 9000-3 does not explicitly mention a quality control organization, in a sense all of ISO 9000 is about the functions and responsibilities of such an organization. But should every type of project have a formal quality control organization? Some say yes; others say that, although it is important that *someone* look out for product (and process) quality, it may be more important for that attention to come from the developers themselves than from a separate, disinterested, overhead-consuming organization.

These issues will recur in the material to follow. Perhaps the strongest statement that can be made here is that large and critical software projects need the formality of separate organizations for each such vital activity. The disagreement that makes this an issue begins after that statement. Should small or noncritical projects have separate configuration management and/or quality control organizations, for example? (In this book, we side with those who advocate formality only where it is necessary, not universally.)

8.7.2 QUALITY ASSURANCE

Quality assurance is the organization that takes outside responsibility for product quality. It is different from *quality design*, which is the activity of the project people themselves to ensure product quality.

The task of this organization is, literally, assurance; it is their job to be sure that quality practices are defined, followed, and documented (the "quality system" is their responsibility). They do not do the quality work itself; typically, they monitor the work to see if the necessary quality practices are being followed.

There are two kinds of quality assurance, process-oriented and product-oriented. Early on in the field, quality assurance was product-oriented. With this kind of quality assurance, quality organization people not only defined procedures and ensured that they were followed, but they also examined the final product, and perhaps intermediate products, to see if the quality they sought was really there.

More recently, quality assurance has evolved into process orientation. Quality assurance people do not examine the final or intermediate products, but rather monitor the processes that should cause the final product to have quality. This new thinking evolves from the notion of statistical process control, wherein data is kept on the successes of various processes, and emphasis is placed on anomalous data that shows that certain processes are not functioning as expected. It also evolves from the work of the Software Engineering Institute on process maturity, wherein software organizations are evaluated on the quality of their software process (this topic is discussed in more depth earlier in this book).

There is still disagreement in the field as to the merit of this evolution. As long as good process leads to good product, the evolution is a good one. But the belief in process is more a manufacturing belief than an engineering belief; it is not at all clear that, in design-oriented disciplines such as software, good process necessarily leads to good product. This disagreement, and a wavering between process- and product-focused quality assurance, will probably continue into the future.

The tasks of the quality organization typically include some or all of these:

- Process metric tracking

- Process improvement

- Reviews and audits (of process or product)

- Product (independent) test

- Configuration management (may be separate)

- Change control (may be separate)

- Contract management (of subcontracts)

- Independent verification and validation

These tasks aggregate into two overall responsibilities:

1. Support to development managers through maintenance (and improvement) of the quality system

2. Support to upper management through monitoring and reporting what is happening in development

8.7.3 CONFIGURATION MANAGEMENT

The task of configuration management is to ensure that there is no way the evolving software product can be lost. This is usually achieved by creating and saving baseline versions of the product from which current versions can be rebuilt if necessary. The product includes not only the code (in various forms, such as source and object), but databases and files, documentation, and any other artifacts essential to the software product.

Configuration management, out of necessity, must take on the task of version control. Typically, software is released to its users/customers in a "version," a variant of the product that is valid at the time of its release for a particular delivery platform, but which may become obsolete as further change is made. Different versions may therefore be platform-dependent (they function on a particular computer or operating system) or chronology-dependent (they are valid at a particular point in time). The number of parameters that are involved in configuration management (artifact, delivery platform, chronology, etc.) is what makes it complicated.

8.7.4 CHANGE CONTROL

Change control is the collection of activities surrounding the changes to the product more than the product itself.
Change control includes:

- Examining change requests to decide on their necessity and importance

- Rejecting changes that do not meet appropriate tests

- Prioritizing changes that pass those tests

- Monitoring change progress to ensure that progress is being made

- Reporting change status to those who have a need to know

- Tracking changes to product versions

- Tracking trends in change activity

8.7.5 CONTRACT MANAGEMENT

If any of the work on the software project must be contracted to another team or enterprise, contract management (also called acquisition management) is necessary. Contract management involves a recursion of all the tasks that make up the total topic of this book. That is, just as this book includes material on the software life-cycle phase activities conducted on behalf of the software project (for example), those same activities are a part of the acquisition process. The one additional task of contract management is to understand the role of the contract in conducting a software project.

Contract management, then, must be focused not only on all the activities in this book, but on what the contract says about them. If the contract says that something must happen, then the contract management team must make sure it happens. Equally important, if the contract does *not* say that something must happen, then it is very unlikely that any amount of contract management can make it happen. (This is the notion of contract "scope"—things that are "in scope" are contractually required, and things that are "out of scope" will not be done unless special consideration is made, i.e., money and schedule relief would be involved.)

Because of the legal implications of contract management, this organization will probably:

- Report higher on the organization chart than comparable development organizations

- Have ongoing interfaces with legal and procurement personnel

8.7.6 PROCESS MANAGEMENT AND IMPROVEMENT

As the quality assurance group has moved from a product focus to a process focus, a special role has evolved for a group specifically devoted to the process used to build the software product. In some companies, this takes the form of a process group. The work of the Software Engineering Institute in defining and measuring process maturity, for example, has spawned individual process groups in enterprises that are involved in that work, and it has also created an infrastructure in which process groups across enterprises meet and discuss topics of their technology on a periodic basis.

The process group typically has these roles:

• Defining the current process baseline

• Defining measures for evaluating process

• Recording the measures for the current process baseline

• Evaluating the measures for any attempted process changes (thus evaluating the process changes themselves)

• Advocating improved process

• Tracking and procuring new technology

• Training software people in new process concepts

• Monitoring the use of new process

8.7.7 METRICS

Metrics are the product of measurement activities. Nearly everyone in the software profession agrees that (a) metrics are desirable, and (b) metrics are seldom used in practice. Beyond those agreements, however, there are vast wallows of disagreement.

The most serious disagreement in metrics is the cleavage between metrics advocated by theory and those advocated by practice. There is little overlap between the two, and as a result it is vital when discussing metrics in a general sense to be very specific about which metrics are being employed. Although metrics are seldom used in practice, there are pockets of success where some very elaborate metrics have been defined and are being employed. Note that the inability of 9000-3 to require specific metrics is related to this problem.

Another disagreement in the metrics field is about what they are for. The problem arises because some see metrics as an end in themselves; in particular, metric theorists see the definition, calculation, and use of metrics as a technical topic. But for most practitioners metrics are clearly a management topic. There may be technology involved in creating and compiling a metric, but the user of that metric is almost undoubtedly going to be a manager. One attempt to better focus on the role of metrics is the "GQM Concept." In that concept, first Goals for metrics are established, then Questions to help achieve those goals are defined, and finally, the Metrics themselves are chosen based on what the questions bring up.

Yet another disagreement about metrics is the lack of a metrics taxonomy. Those who see metrics as an end in themselves especially tend to lump all metrics together. However, a common taxonomy of metrics divides them into process metrics and product metrics. Process metrics are usually about prediction; based on past performance of some task, such as detecting errors in the software, we predict that future performance of that task will have these characteristics. Product metrics are usually about quality; based on some sort of examination, product quality (e.g., the reliability of the product) is given a certain value. Process metrics, in addition to being about reliability prediction, are often about cost and schedule prediction. Product metrics, in addition to being about reliability, may also be about performance, or maintainability, or any of the quality attributes.

The importance of metrics is that, through their use, we can form conclusions about the goodness or badness of some aspects of software development and maintenance. How else could we, for example, measure the costs and benefits of some new technology, such as object-oriented approaches or client/server delivery systems? Ironically, not only is the use of metrics rare in practice to date, but software researchers rarely employ them either. There is very little data about the goodness or badness of new technologies emerging from the research world. It is easy to criticize both software practice and software research for failing to study and use appropriate metrics.

That situation will probably change in the near future. One agent of change will be ISO 9000 itself - although it punts on what metrics should be used to develop and maintain software, it at least requires them to be defined and used. Similarly, the higher levels of the Software Engineering Institute Capability (Process) Maturity Model demand the use of metrics to evaluate process. And finally, the U.S. Department of Defense has recently required that certain software projects, such as those involving embedded systems, must define and use metrics.

Change is likely in the research world as well. Attacks on the current practice of "advocacy research"—research where a new technology is advocated based on no evaluative evidence of its costs and benefits—are increasing, and it is likely that at least some increasing attempts to include measurement as part of the software research process will result.

8.7.8 DOCUMENTATION

Software documentation is a many-faceted concept. In the course of developing and maintaining a software product, there are probably two dozen documents that may or may not be required.

Some of those documents are created to assist in the management of the software process, some are created because of their technical value to the software developers, and some are created to assist the customer or user. Plans, for example, are typically management documentation. Phase-ending documents, although they are useful to management for showing progress, are more commonly technical documentation to support the technical handoff process. User manuals and installation documents are examples of user-focused documents.

There is seldom a discussion of the relative importance of these documents, and that may be unfortunate. For example, customer-/user-oriented documentation is usually vital;

a software product cannot be useful without it. Technical documentation may be slightly less vital, but, on the other hand, it is difficult to build a software product without an agreed-upon requirements specification, thorough design documentation, and even more thorough and correct maintenance documentation. There is irony in the fact that although most texts on software engineering (and ISO 9000 itself!) place the strongest emphasis on management-related documents, they are probably the least necessary in the overall history of a software project. Of course, for large or critical projects, plans and procedures and reports are still vital; but they are considerably more expendable toward the smaller, noncritical end of the spectrum.

8.7.9 SUPPORTING ACTIVITIES SUMMARY

ISO 9000-3 discusses a variety of topics for software's supporting activities: configuration management, document control, quality records, measurement, "rules, practices, and conventions," tools and techniques, purchasing, "included software product," and training. It is a broad and useful list, and 9000-3 has one or more requirements for each of the topics in the list.

Here, probably more than for any other facet of software construction, judgment must be applied to the way in which the 9000-3 requirements are achieved. Formal document control, for example, is necessary on large projects but can choke small ones. Tools and techniques which might be procured on behalf of a large project may only be borrowed, or not used at all, on smaller ones. It is not that the requirements of 9000-3 should be ignored; instead, it is important to find appropriate ways to satisfy them, and those ways should be dependent on the type of project.

In this section, we have chosen to address supporting activities in a somewhat different manner from that defined by 9000-3. We have tried to aggregate the activities of 9000-3 into typical organizational entities in the industrial project environment. For example, some of the 9000-3 concepts map directly into the sections above on:

- Configuration management

- Measurement (metrics)

- Document control (documentation)

Others require a more involved mapping:

- Quality records, "rules, practices and conventions," tools and techniques (quality assurance)

- Purchasing, "included software product" (contract management)

And one is not covered at all:

- Training

There is no doubt that training is vital for software project people. Often training is provided by the organization rather than on a project, although for large and critical projects specialized training may be required. We believe in training; we do not mention it because, in this case, we believe 9000-3 speaks nicely for itself.

As can be seen in Table 8.6, the strongest determiner of using formal approaches to the supporting activities is project size. Large projects tend to need all the supporting activities, formally applied, that are available. Similarly, critical projects also tend to need formal approaches. But innovative projects often need little formality; formal approaches tend to add cost and time to a project, and innovative projects should be much more focused on following through on the innovation than on formality. As can also be seen in the table, the application domain has little to do with these supporting activities.

Table 8.6 Project Types vs. Techniques: Supporting Activities

Technique/Tool	Project Type:									
	Size		Application				Criticality		Innova-tiveness	
	Lg	Sm	Bus	Sci	Sys	R-T	High	Low	High	Low
Quality Assurance	F	I	<--see lg, sm				F	I	I	<-
Configuration Management	F	I	<--see lg, sm				F	I	I	<-
Change Control	F	I	<--see lg, sm				F	I	I	<-
Contract Management	IN	IN	IN	IN	IN	IN	IN	IN	IN	IN
Process Management and Improvement	Y	N	<--see lg, sm				Y	N	N	N
Metrics	Y	N	<--see lg, sm				Y	N	N	N
Documentation	F	I	<--see lg, sm				F	I	I	I

Legend:
F = Formal
I = Informal
IN =If needed
N = No
Y = Yes
<- = Defer to type at left

SUMMARY

Quality is an elusive topic. We have problems defining it. We have problems achieving it. We have problems measuring it. Over the years, the pursuit of quality has taxed the finest minds applied to the topic. We have even seen major differences between nations, and metamorphoses of nations, as they have wrestled with the quality of their products.

Software quality is an even more elusive topic. Definitional problems are multiplied. Sometimes motivating it takes precedence over achieving it. Measurement efforts have largely failed over the years—academic and practitioner attempts to measure quality, for example, differ profoundly. And there is enormous difference of opinion as to how much quality the software profession has really achieved in its products.

Into that morass and void steps ISO 9000. It provides an internationally mandated attempt to define and provide for product quality in the customer-supplier relationship, and it adds on some specific thinking about software quality. Certainly, those who breathed life into the standard deserve at least rewards for bravery!

But do they deserve rewards for a major contribution to

the field? Here, particularly for software, things become less clear.

In this book, we have given two different answers to that question. An overwhelming "yes" answer is given by Östen Oskarsson, who says "I *love* ISO 9000," and proceeds, through his knowledge and experience, to give some excellent reasons for his belief in it. It is easy to accept his viewpoint that the standard is essential to the customer who wants to ensure purchasing a quality software product.

But the second answer is an unenthusiastic "No." Robert L. Glass says, "The more I read [about the standard], the less interested I became." He goes on to tell of his early struggles with the usefulness of the standard, given his own belief that software quality is fundamentally a technical topic, and ISO 9000 is about managing for quality.

Is it possible to blend these disparate views? Have we, now that we have reached the end of their joint book on ISO 9000, seen any resolution of this fundamental disagreement? Or is this book the personification of the odd couple, two friends working together despite the gulf of a fundamental disagreement between them?

Finding a blending of these viewpoints is a matter of really understanding what the standard is. As we have seen earlier in the book, there are three important things to remember about ISO 9000:

1. It is a tool for buyers, not builders.

2. It is about what, not how.

3. It provides necessary, but not sufficient, direction.

Given that understanding, most of the early Glass objections to the standard are eased, if not eliminated.

But there is a problem with this understanding. In the typical rush of the computing field to jump on whatever bandwagons happen along, software enthusiasts have jumped uncritically aboard ISO 9000 and made its use the latest "breakthrough" concept for improving the field. Most such enthusiasts do not understand the three points above. And in that lack of understanding, great mischief is once again being done to the software field.

That brings us to the real point of this summary section of the book. What should the reader remember as the back cover looms ever closer in the page-turning process? Certainly, the first and most important thing to remember is the true nature of what ISO 9000 is—and is not. Östen Oskarsson is right when he says "I love ISO 9000." Robert L. Glass is right when he says "The more I read, the less interested I became." The blending of these apparently schizophrenic views is a matter of adjusting expectations, getting a clear picture of what ISO 9000 is intended to accomplish. The standard accomplishes nicely what it set out to accomplish. It should not be pushed to accomplish more than that.

What else should the reader remember? Here is a collection of the authors' favorite ideas from the book. Our hope is that you will take at least these ideas, and preferably many more, with you when you close the back cover at last.

The first part of the book is presented by Oskarsson. He makes several important points:

1. ISO 9000 is a family of international quality standards. One member of that family, ISO 9001, is for products that require design. A special interpretation of 9001, 9000-3, has been prepared for software because of the important uniquenesses of software.

2. The basic message of ISO 9000-3 is twofold:
   a. All operations influencing quality shall be under control.
   b. That control shall be visible.

3. There are two ways to meet the requirements of 9001:
   a. Issue a procedure and check to see that it is followed.
   b. Assign responsibility and authority to a competent person.

4. Quality control shall be provided through a quality system. Such a system comprises "the organizational structure, reponsibilities, procedures, processes and resources for implementing quality management."

5. The achievement of ISO certification is an important and well understood process. That process is described in detail earlier in the book. Although some have characterized the fundamentals of meeting the standard by the phrase "When in doubt, document," it is important to remember that achievement can be thwarted by "bureaucratic personalities who mistake paper for products."

6. ISO 9000 exists in a milieu of other quality efforts. A British process called TickIT has been defined to serve as a standard for the ISO software certification process. But such competing standards as those of the Software Engineering Institute and its five-level Capability Maturity Model and the U.S. DoD's own software standards must be considered by an organization seeking to provide assurance of its software quality efforts. The book provides some guidelines for understanding when each is important.

7. Experience with ISO 9000 software certification identifies some common organizational problems and concerns, such as the roles of the standard for R&D software, prototyping efforts, and legacy software. These and other topics are discussed in depth.

8. Some rules of thumb for the process are provided, including:
   a. To build a quality system, use quality people and make sure that the results are technically viable. If you do, the technical software people will accept the system with few reservations.
   b. To achieve certification, be patient. A quality system should be used for awhile, and its bugs wrung out, so that at certification time there are credibility-building experiences with the use of the system to present.

The last part of the book, written by Glass, also makes several important points:

1. Applying ISO 9000 to a software project is no small task.

2. Gaps must be filled between the standard's "what" and a practical "how," and the standard's "necessary" and a much more complex "sufficient." In fact, achieving "how" and "sufficient" often causes "what" and "necessary" to be modified.

3. The achievement of software quality must be accomplished differently for different types of projects. For that purpose, in this book projects are categorized as to their
   a. Size
   b. Application domain
   c. Criticality
   d. Innovativeness
   Such a categorization is a new concept in this book, one not yet well accepted in the field. Practitioners will have an easier time accepting this idea than theoreticians, who have traditionally sought "one-size-fits-all" technical approaches.

4. The bulk of this material describes each of the life-cycle phases as defined by ISO 9000, in terms of what the standard requires, what unresolved issues confront the field for that phase, what technologies and tools are available to assist in the achievement of quality in that phase, and a comparison/contrast of what the standard requires vs. what good practice requires. A table is provided for each life-cycle phase, showing for what types of projects each of the techniques/tools is effective. In total, over five dozen technologies/tools are discussed.

5. The treatment of those five dozen technologies/tools in this book assumes that the reader understands something about them already. If the reader needs more depth, he or she is advised to read further in the book

Building Quality Software (Prentice Hall, 1992), which is a companion volume to this one, organized in a similar fashion.

6. Software design choices are characterized in a two-dimensional matrix, where the designer will select an approach based on this layout:

	Top-down	Bottom-up	Hard-part-first
Process			
Data			
Object			
Event			

Choice of a row in the matrix is most dependent on application domain. Choice of a column is dependent on many things, but in fact the most effective approach is recommended as "top-down overview, bottom-up reusable modules, and then proceed hard-part-first."

7. Software testing is characterized as a multifaceted process, defined by this layout:

	Unit test	Integration test	System test
Require-ments-driven			
Structure-driven			
Risk-driven			
Statistics-driven			

Unlike the matrix for design above, good testing involves accomplishing most of the tasks implied by the cells of the matrix.

8. Differences between what ISO 9000-3 requires and what good software practice requires are sometimes profound. The biggest differences lie in the requirements, design/implementation, testing/validation, and maintenance phases. The smallest differences lie in the "replication/delivery/installation" phase. But oddly, ISO 9000-3 has as much to say about the latter phase as about the more complicated ones.

9. The book takes some especially controversial positions. It recommends against formal verification (proof of correctness) for all projects, even those that are critical. This advice flies in the face of a legal requirement by the British Ministry of Defense to use formal techniques on embedded, real-time software applications. It recommends the use of postdelivery reviews, which are seldom employed in practice, and the use of structure-driven testing, which must be supported by a tool known as the "test coverage analyzer," one seldom used in the field.

And there we have it. In sum, we, the authors, think we have here a book that is:

- Mainstream, yet contrarian

- Supportive of ISO 9000, while soundly criticizing it

- Full of ideas the reader already knows, while suggesting concepts rarely used in practice and not well understood in theory

- Framed by familiar and traditional life-cycle concepts, while providing structure to those concepts never presented elsewhere

- Most of all, rich with the experiences of a couple of software authors who have "been there" and "done that" in the field of software quality!

INDEX

D

E